*Mughals, Maharajas
and the Mahatma*

Mughals, Maharajas and the Mahatma

K.R.N. SWAMY

HarperCollins *Publishers* India

HarperCollins *Publishers* India Pvt Ltd
7/16 Ansari Road, Daryaganj, New Delhi 110 002

© K.R.N. Swamy 1997

Published 1997 by
HarperCollins *Publishers* India
Second impression 1998

K.R.N. Swamy asserts the moral right
to be identified as the author of this work

ISBN 81-7223-280-2

Cover Design: Bitten Nails
Illustrations: Tapas Guha

Typeset by
Megatechnics
19A, Ansari Road
New Delhi 110 002

Printed in India by
Gopsons Papers Ltd
A-14, Sector 60
Noida 201 301

To my wife
Smt. Janaki Swamy
as but for her loving care, this book
would not have been written

Introduction

While doing research on Indian history, especially in such hallowed libraries like the National Archives of India and the India Office Library, London, one often comes across nuggets of information or few phrases in the documents, which entices one to do further 'pursue' these 'forgotten pages of history'. The book 'Mughals, Maharajas and the Mahatma' comprises of thirty-nine such episodes based on such slivers of history.

To paraphrase the eminent historian, late Sir Jadu Nath Sarkar's advise to his disciple Dr. Raghbir Singh, writing history is like assembling pieces of mosaic, sort of solving a jigsaw puzzle. Some pieces of the mosaic may not be available — to be completed later by future historians.

All the included articles have been published in prestigious journals in India and abroad. My only regret is that, my 50 years old collection of newspaper clippings and archival materials collected from libraries all over the world were irretrievably damaged by the heavy rains on 10th June 1990 — the heaviest monsoon downpour Bombay experienced in the past one hundred years. Otherwise all the episodes would have been followed with necessary references/foot notes/bibliography/index.

Mughals, Maharajas and the Mahatma

Providentially for me, my wife Smt. Janaki Swamy had kept one copy each of my published articles in our flat. But for her care, there would have been no record left of my freelance writing in Indian history since 1954. Hence I dedicate this book to my beloved wife Smt. Janaki Swamy.

August 1997   K.R.N. Swamy

List of Illustrations

The Treasures of the Indian Maharajas
    Bharatpur Maharaja's Rolls Royce   4
    Nizam of Hyderabad Jewellery   5
    Patiala Maharaja's aigrette   8
    Silver Elephant Chair of Baroda Ruler   11
    The Indore 'Pear' Diamonds   12

The Parthenon and the Taj Mahal
    The Parthenon Today   19

Fabulous Thrones of India
    Traditional Gaddi/Masnad of Kota Maharaja   28
    Throne of Tipu Sultan   29
    Tiger head filial of Tipu Sultan's Throne   29
    Throne of Maharaja Ranjit Singh   31
    Silver Thrones of Delhi Durbar   34

The English East India Company
    Coat of Arms, English East India Company   46
    Queen Victoria in 1877   52

How They Met the Mahatma
    Nehru, Gandhi & Patel

1914: When German Warship Emden *Planned to Liberate Indian Patriots from the Andamans*
    German light cruiser *Emden*   77

A British Viceroy's Tribute to a Mughal Empress
    Lord Curzon   81

Treasures of the Last Peshwa
    Nana Saheb Peshwa   87

The Sepoy Mutiny of 1857 as seen by Queen Victoria
    Cartridge that caused the Sepoy Mutiny   93
    Queen Victoria in 1857   94

The Martyr-Emperor's Unfulfilled Wish
    Last Mughal Bahadur Shah exiled   102

Indian Maharajas: 'After Ambassadors, Before Dukes'
    Maharaja Sajjan Singh of Mewar   110
    Maharaja Ranjit Singh of Nawanagar   118

A British View of the Jallianwala Bagh Massacre
    General Dyer   121

The World's Seventh Largest Diamond
    The Nizam — buyer of Jacob Diamond   127

The Queen who wanted to be an Empress
    New Crowns for Old — *Times* Cartoon   143

When the Maharana of Udaipur Threatened to Commit Suicide
    Maharana Fateh Singh of Udaipur   154
    Heraldic shield of Maharana of Udaipur   157

List of Illustrations

Jawaharlal Nehru and the Maharajas
    Nehru and the Nizam of Hyderabad   164

Mahatma Gandhi and Adolf Hitler
    Mahatma Gandhi   167
    Hitler   170

Muslin — The Fabric that Ruined its Weavers
    Muslin emroidered with silver wire   181

They Wanted to Build Another Taj Mahal
    Black Taj Mahal & White Taj Mahal   185
    Shah Jahan and Mumtaj Mahal   186

Men who Ruled the Maharajas
    British Residency at Hyderabad   199

The Great White Mutiny
    Lord Ripon   210

An Indian Patriot in British Parliament
    Dadabhai Naoroji   223

Mahatma Gandhi — Historians Delve into the Mystery of his Leadership
    Mahatma Gandhi   232

The Title Maharajas Could Not Buy
    His Highness the Begum of Bhopal   238

Contents

Introduction vii
List of Illustrations ix

1. The Treasures of the Indian Maharajas — 1
2. The Parthenon and the Taj Mahal — 16
3. Mahatma Gandhi's Gift to Queen Elizabeth — 23
4. Fabulous Thrones of India — 27
5. Mahatma Gandhi, Einstein and the Atom Bomb — 37
6. The 'Lost' Bible — 41
7. The English East India Company — 45
8. The Costliest Treasure in History — 54
9. The Mahatma's Encounters with British Statesmen — 58
10. How They Met the Mahatma — 66
11. 1914: When German Warship *Emden* Planned to Liberate Indian Patriots from the Andamans — 74
12. A British Viceroy's Tribute to a Mughal Empress — 80
13. Treasures of the Last Peshwa — 86
14. The Sepoy Mutiny of 1857 as seen by Queen Victoria — 91
15. The Martyr-Emperor's Unfulfilled Wish — 100

16	October 2, 1869: The Day Mahatma Gandhi was born	106
17	Indian Maharajas: 'After Ambassadors, Before Dukes'	109
18	A British View of the Jallianwala Bagh Massacre	120
19	The World's Seventh Largest Diamond	126
20	When Mahatma Gandhi Met King George V at Buckingham Palace	133
21	The Queen who wanted to be an Empress	140
22	Delhi Durbar 1911 — The Grandest Pageant of the Century	147
23	When the Maharana of Udaipur Threatened to Commit Suicide	153
24	Jawaharlal Nehru and the Maharajas	159
25	Mahatma Gandhi and Adolf Hitler	166
26	A Portion of India That Will Always be Burma	172
27	Muslin — The Fabric that Ruined its Weavers	180
28	They Wanted to Build Another Taj Mahal	184
29	Danish Castle on Indian Shores	191
30	Men who Ruled the Maharajas	195
31	It was Jawaharlal Nehru's Birthday	204
32	The Great White Mutiny	209
33	An Indian Patriot in British Parliament	222
34	Mahatma Gandhi — Historians Delve into the Mystery of his Leadership	230
35	The Title Maharajas Could Not Buy	236
36	The Greatest Plunder in History	242
37	When Indian Patriots Wanted an Indian Officer Corps for the Indian Army	248
38	Indian Independence, Nehru and Hitler	255
39	British Ghosts Continue to Haunt India	260

Acknowledgments

A book of historical episodes like this could not be written without the help of scholars and librarians of important libraries. My thanks are especially due to Dr. R.K. Perti — till recently the Director General of the National Archives of India, New Delhi, late Dr. L.P. Sihare the Director General of the National Museum of India, New Delhi, the librarians of the newspaper division of the British Library, London, the Theosophical Society Library and Research Centre at Adyar, Madras, Heras Society Library at Bombay, the Nehru Memorial Library at New Delhi and the Directors of the British Naval Museum at Portsmouth, UK.

The Treasures of the Indian Maharajas

The very first maharaja Europe had seen was Maharaja Duleep Singh of the Punjab, who, in the 1850s graced Queen Victoria's court, resplendent in his magnificent jewels, which formed but a small portion of his heritage, as the last titular ruler of the Punjab. For the next hundred years, the Indian maharajas dazzled the Western world with their legendary treasures and fabulously large jewels. Ropes of pearls, beautiful cabochon gems of varied hue, often engraved with flowers and inscriptions, and the fabled Golconda diamonds, with their snowflake appeal and ethereal dispersion of light, all caught the bemused eye of the world.

As vassals of the British sovereign, the maharajas gifted priceless treasures to the royal family, and the British writer Suzy Menkes in her book *British Crown Jewels,* states that till the maharajas entered the scene as 'gift givers,' Queen Victoria figured low on the list of European royalty when it came to jewellery. She states that even today, the huge quantities of treasure given to the British monarch and the successive Princes of Wales, is not officially listed and that only Garrards, the royal jewellers, have the unofficial list, which they are not willing to disclose.

In the winter of 1947, as the newly independent India, a barely three-months-old renascent nation, was struggling to find its feet, the intelligence department of the Government of India brought news to Sardar Patel, the Home Minister, that the Indian maharajas were melting down centuries-old family heirlooms like elephant howdahs (sofas), in order to convert the treasures into saleable bullion. The indomitable Sardar, known as the Iron Man of India, achieved a remarkable feat in negotiating the accession of 565 Princely States to India — a greater task than the one undertaken by Bismarck, the 'Iron' Chancellor of Germany, who welded the Germanic States into a single nation in the 1870s. Sardar Patel had promised the maharajas generous Privy Purses and the right to retain their private wealth. The Sardar was not disturbed by the news, 'Right now, I am interested in creating a unified India with the help of the Indian Princes', he answered, 'the question of taking action for their destroying national heirlooms, will come later.'

In 1947-48, as the Indian States Ministry integrated the 565 Indian princedoms into the Indian Union, it had divided the jewellery of the princes into two categories — one, State Regalia such as thrones, crowns and other items acquired for the particular state from state funds and secondly, jewellery acquired privately by the rulers with their own funds. The lists had then been handed over to the last Secretary of the Indian States Ministry, C.S. Venkatachar.

But decades later, in the late 1980s, an eminent Indian museologist, the Director General of the National Museum of India at Delhi, Dr. L.P. Sihare, discovered that only very minor treasures and jewellery had been listed under State Regalia and most of the precious jewellery had been categorized as the private property of the various Indian maharajas. The Nizam of Hyderabad, for instance (the richest man in the world in 1945, according to *Readers' Digest*), possessing over a thousand million US dollars worth of treasures, had in 1950, submitted a list of over 1800 gems and jewellery items, claiming them to be his private property (valued at Rs. 120,000,000). The State Regalia, however, listed only 26 most insignificant items, valued at Rs. 4,000,000! Similarly, the Maharaja of Baroda (the eighth richest man in the world during the pre-war years) declared a mere Rs. 3,600,000 worth of State jewellery; the Maharaja of Mysore, Rs. 2,500,000 worth; the Maharaja of Jaipur priced his state treasures at Rs. 13,000,000 and the ruler of Indore sent in a list of heirlooms valued at Rs. 10,000,000.

The so called 'personal wealth', which the maharajas were to retain, was meticulously recorded. As per the list prepared for one of them, the Maharaja of Jaipur, the personal property included:

The City Palace, with all the treasures in it; the Jaipur City square, with the Town Hall and surrounding buildings; Rambagh Palace, including outhouses; all buildings within the Palace compound; historical mansions (numbering 200 and inclusive of the fortresses of Jaigarh and Hathroi); two polo grounds; horse paddocks; 10 temples; two shooting lodges in the forests with outhouses and surrounding grounds; 83,300 acres of uncultivated land for farming; supply of hay and fodder to ponies and cattle; and 19,000 acres of grasslands.

All articles in the buildings, such as fitments, furniture, hangings, books, photographs, pictures and paintings, electric and sanitary appliances, trophies, watches, cutlery and crockery, glass and silverware, centre pieces, bronzes, flower vases, all the art treasures, old arms and jewellery gold coins numbering 140,000 and primary gold weighing 640 lb.

A Ford, Pontiac, Delahaye, Rover, Studebaker, Packard, Hillman station wagon, Chevrolet truck, Chevrolet lorry,

Bharatpur Maharaja's Rolls Royce

Cadillacs(2), Bentleys(3), Buicks(6), Rolls Royces(3), Chevrolets(3), Hillmans(2), Austins(4), Vauxhalls(3), Morrises(2), Humbers, Oldsmobiles, Jeeps(8), Command Cars, Chevrolet vans(2), Ford trucks.

Horse carriages(26), Polo ponies 94 (with saddlery, etc), one coach with four horses, horses(50), one elephant carriage and all the paraphernalia of gold and silver ornaments, saddlery and caparisons for elephants, horses, camels and bullocks.

Decades later, in 1995, the dispute between members of the Jaipur royal family served to bring to the notice of the Jaipur High Court the actual list of 'personal wealth', hidden from the Government of India in 1947. The Maharaja of Jaipur died in 1967 leaving behind three wives. The third wife, Dowager Maharani Gayatri Devi and her sons, challenged the eldest son of the first wife over a 150-page list of palaces, jewellery, paintings and other royal possessions estimated at US $ 322 million. Most of the family's jewels, paintings and carpets remain sealed in six strong rooms and 17 warehouses by order of the Jaipur High Court, as the legal tug-of-war with the State and Central Governments continues for possession of palaces and lands valued at hundreds of millions of dollars. After all, till the 1900s, all the area that comprises India's capital of New Delhi, belonged to the Jaipur royal family! An ironic sequel was that, despite all these treasures, in 1977 Indira Gandhi, then Prime Minister of India, sought to arrest her political rival, the Dowager Maharani Gayatri Devi of Jaipur, for possessing without permit, a paltry sum of £ 17.

In order to gain a brief idea of the priceless treasures which were (and at least some of which still are) with various former rulers, a few of them can be highlighted:

The De Beer Diamond (cut weight 234 carats, worth over Rs. 300 million, owned by the Maharaja of Patiala); the famous seven-strand pearl necklace of the Maharaja of Baroda, estimated value about Rs. 3.6 millions in 1903; four world-famous diamonds: Star of the South (125 carats), Eugene (51 carats), Akbar Shah (72 carats) and the English Dresden (76½ carats) — all purchased in the late 1860s by the late Malhar Rao Gaekwar of Baroda at the cost of £80,000, £15,000, £35,000 and £40,000, respectively (owned by the heirs of the Maharaja of Baroda); the fabulous multi-strand pearl necklace of the Maharaja Scindia of Gwalior with 12,000 priceless pearls; the famous Nizam diamond (227 carats) and the Jacob

Nizam of Hyderabad's Jewellery

Diamond (184.5 carats) worth over Rs. 700 million and Rs. 400 million respectively, and the collection of exquisite emeralds worth about Rs. 600 million, all owned by the Nizam of Hyderabad; the three famous emeralds, the largest of which is 490 carats, and a necklace of three rows of spinel rubies 'each as large as a bantam hen's egg', which originally belonged to the 16th century Mughal Emperor Babur and are now owned by the heirs to the Maharaja of Jaipur.

Besides such famous gems, also available are details of sizeable and exquisite State jewellery and several renowned Regalia items such as the Jahangir Nazarana Gold Coin and the Shah Jahan Nazarana Gold coin (weighing over 11 kg and 1 kg respectively) for which the highest bid of US $ 8.5 million was received in Switzerland in 1987; the Baroda Royal Pearl Carpet, which was offered for sale in Geneva for US $ 31 million in 1989, and the Baroda three-pounder gun, made of solid gold, weighing a little over 95 kg.

Another consideration was whether the treasures were outside India on the midnight of August 14 when the maharajas were still independent rulers. If the treasures had been taken out before then the Indian Government had no legal authority to ask for their return. Fifty years after Indian independence, literally millions of rupees worth of national treasures left in the custody of the erstwhile Indian princes have been sold abroad. It is probable that nearly twenty thousand million US dollars worth of national treasure has been smuggled out of India in the past five decades, a high percentage belonging to the Indian princes.

The first instance that came to light of these fabulous treasures being disposed of abroad was in 1954, when the Maharaja of Burdwan was fined a huge amount for trying to sell the famous centuries-old Jahangir diamond at a public auction by the London firm of Sotheby's. In the ensuing court case, however, the Government of India discovered that it had not officially intimated the maharajas that any item over a hundred years old could not be sold outside India without the permission of the Indian Government. The fine was refunded.

Again in the 1950s and 60s, information continued to reach the Indian Government that valuable treasures belonging to the erstwhile Indian princes were being sold clandestinely to famous international jewellers. These treasures had been acquired by the maharajas as family heirlooms, over the centuries, and furthermore during the British period, especially between 1900 and 1930s, with the revenue from the states they governed, when huge amounts were appropriated from the taxes paid by their subjects.

Evidence from the Boucheron Jewellers Archives states that the 1929 exposition at the Musee Galliera, in Paris, where the Patiala jewels (entrusted to the firm of Boucheron for remodelling) were displayed, was a landmark in the jewellery world. Documents from the Boucheron Archives state, 'When the Maharaja of Patiala debarked at a hotel on the Champs-Elysees, with a retinue of forty servants and his twenty favourite dancing girls, Parisians were somewhat amazed. He was accompanied by cascades of diamonds, rubies, emeralds and other precious stones enclosed in six metal chests and protected by a dozen tall guards. The Potentate showed Baron Fouquier, the Boucheron representative this hoard of precious stones, wrapped very simply in coloured diaphanous fabrics and in the Baron's words, "My breathless admiration was never-to-be-forgotten. First white, then yellow and bluish diamonds appeared, followed by pearls and the most magnificent collection of emeralds imaginable. Last of all were the sapphires and rubies"'.

The value of this treasure was estimated at 1,800,000,000 francs in 1929. The re-mounting of the gems, in particular 1,800 carats of emeralds, the most beautiful ever assembled,

Patiala Maharaja's Aigrette

was most impressive. There was a cascading necklace worth 150,000,000 francs on its own: another of woven and cascading diamonds, with pear-shaped emeralds of exceptional quality and three very ancient plaquettes. Finally, the Maharani of Patiala's jewel — a fringe of diamonds and emeralds worn beneath a sari — provided the proper mysterious effect. An emerald armband worn on the left arm, was the crowning decorative insignia of the Maharaja of Patiala's rank: the central emerald weighed 100 carats and was surrounded by diamonds and cascading pear-shaped emeralds. However, it was the insignia of the Maharani of Patiala's rank — a diamond crescent with a star in large rubies — that drew everyone's attention.

The irony of the situation was that at the same time, the Maharaja of Patiala was desperately trying to obtain a loan of £ 2,000,000 from the Government of India to clear his long outstanding debts. In order to 'save the face' of a premier Indian maharaja, the Government of India finally granted the loan, having first appointed a Financial Controller to prevent the repetition of such requests.

The 1930s also saw the Maharaja of Darbhanga buying the fabulous Marie Antoinette necklace. Made with 647 stones, weighing 2,800 carats, this fabulous necklace was known to be in the vaults of the Maharaja in the 1960s. Of course, many of the diamonds had been extracted from the necklace in the aftermath of the French revolution. It was, nevertheless, one of the national treasures of France. But a 1982 search revealed that the register listing the jewels taken out of the Darbhanga family treasure vaults by the Maharani for festival occasions, was 'missing' and so were the fabulous jewels of the Darbhanga family. In fact, the list of the Darbhanga jewels kept by the jeweller's firm of Van Cleef & Arpels had to be invoked to know what was missing.

But after Indian independence, the priceless treasures were sold off. To quote one incident, from the official history of the fabulous French jeweller's firm of Van Cleef & Arpels, 'In complete secrecy, on information supplied by one of his numerous correspondents scattered all over the world, the jeweller himself departs in the hope of acquiring unique and sometimes legendary stones'. Claude Arpels must certainly have been in a state close to exaltation, when in 1956, he acquired the *Neela Rani* (also called the Blue Princess), belonging to an Indian maharaja, from a Bombay dealer. It was an incomparable sapphire of 114 carats which became, in 1965, at Florence J Gould's request, the central motif of a necklace, combined with three other important sapphires edged with diamonds and linked with baguette sapphires.

Claude Arpels had also the privilege, the same year, of meeting the Maharaja Sahib Bahadur of Rewa, who wished to dispose of certain stones. Conforming with the custom which forbade a maharaja to enter into direct negotiations with a prospective buyer, Claude Arpels asked a British colonel to act as intermediary. Arriving at Rewa, he had to wait for several days until the Maharaja had consulted his astrologer.

After seeing the treasures, Claude Arpels returned to New Delhi and acquired the fabulous Rewa Collection which included a fantastic cabochon emerald of more than 100 carats; two priceless necklaces of the kind worn by maharajas on rare occasions — one comprised of 55 emeralds set in a lattice of diamonds and pearls, from which hung an emerald of exceptional size, and the other a lattice of white diamonds embellished in the middle by a pink diamond, extremely rare in India; a *Nauratan* necklace tiara comprising of nine varieties of priceless precious stones (emerald, ruby, blue sapphire, yellow sapphire, cat's eye, topaz, coral and diamond and a single pearl), representing the nine planets of the Indian zodiac, which Hindu princes wear to protect themselves from harmful influences; a collection of bangles with enamel work, set with precious stones, depicting dragon or elephant heads, and flexible bracelets intended to adorn the forearm. This collection of jewels was shown to a privileged few at the Plaza Hotel in New York in March 1956.

Claude Arpels also made a visit to the Maharaja of Jamnagar but one does not know whether the fabulous necklace of diamonds, rubies and emeralds created for the famous cricketer, Maharaja Ranjit Singhji of Jamnagar, in the 1920s (described by the eminent French jeweller's firm of Cartier as the most precious necklace in the world in the 1930s), is still in India. From the Maharaja of Lunawada, Arpels acquired one of the most sumptuous diamond necklaces he had ever seen.

Confronted with a situation where the country was losing fabulous treasures and yet not gaining in foreign exchange, the Government of India in the 1960s decided to allow the export of heirlooms, provided the foreign exchange earned was brought back to India. This permission resulted in a veritable avalanche of various State Regalia leaving India. For example, in the 1970s, we find Sotheby's advertising the sale of the fabulous State Elephant howdah (sofa) of the Gaekwars of Baroda, in Germany. In another instance, an Australian antique dealer arrived in Mysore in southern India, to buy many valuable curios from the treasures of the Maharajas of Mysore — till the infuriated citizens of Mysore forced a halt to the sale.

Similarly in the 1960s, *Blitz* of Bombay, reported the 'disappearance' of the famous pearls from the Nawab of

Silver Elephant Chair of the Baroda Ruler

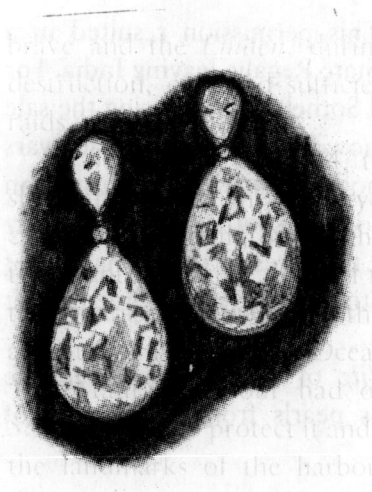

The Indore 'Pear' Diamond

Rampur's collection.

Such magical stones as the sensational Indore pear-shaped diamonds of 46 carats and 44 carats, had also vanished in the market. The Maharaja of Indore was wont to wear these as ornaments and the two diamonds were the star pieces of a 1987 Christie's auction in Geneva where they were knocked down to a Middle Eastern buyer for US $ 2,688,000.

But, when in 1991, the fabulous jewels of the Nizam of Hyderabad came up for sale, Indian museologists, led by the late Dr. L.P. Sihare, banded together and succeeded in blocking the sale of the jewels. These jewels, a 37 piece collection, valued at about US $ 65 million (in 1995), by the arbitrator appointed by the Government of India and at US $ 465 million by the heirs to the last Nizam (who died in 1967), have been acquired for the National Museum at New Delhi by the Government of India. The costliest item in the collection is the Jacob diamond, weighing 184.75 carats and reckoned to be the world's third best in whiteness and seventh in size.

At times, the keepers of these treasures go to great lengths in order to ensure they remain hidden. Maneka Gandhi, daughter-in-law of the late Prime Minister Indira Gandhi, working as a journalist, had carte blanche to visit any place in India and once visited the fabulous Faluknuma Palace belonging to the Nizams of Hyderabad, and which is normally not open to any persons outside the Nizam's family. While passing through the grand drawing room, where, since the early 1910s, US $ 12 million worth of curios are kept in show cases, she saw a beautiful miniature gold peacock with a diamond, ruby and emerald-studded feather train. She expressed delight at such a fine example of the jeweller's art and as she concluded her tour of the palace, wished to have one more look at the peacock. But the peacock was missing! Her enquiries elicited only the vaguest response. Obviously scared, the guardians of the palace apparently felt that she may ask for the piece as a souvenir of her visit, and had prudently removed it.

Many of the treasures did not go to London, but were sold by auction in Europe with Switzerland as a base. The Indian press was not fully geared to report such sales in Europe, whereas in London there existed a full corps of Indian correspondents. The treasures were mainly bought by rich Americans and Japanese. It was easier to get the valuables directly to the US from Europe than through the stricter and more knowledgeable British Customs, who could inform the Government of India.

One major bid in 1977 was for the family dinner service of the Patiala maharajas. This could not be sold as the auction price did not reach the reserve price of £ 200,000.

A treasure recently lost to India has been the Pearl Carpet of the Maharajas of Baroda. In the 1947-1948 period, the then Maharaja of Baroda, Sir Pratap Singh Rao Gaekwar, had taken it out of India and after his death it passed into the hands of his Maharani, Sita Devi, who still resides at Monte Carlo. Efforts by the Government of India to regain the carpet, priced in 1989 at US $ 31 million, were in vain and it was thought to be kept in a bank vault in Geneva. Its history is interesting and the last time the general public saw it was during the Delhi Durbar of 1903, when the then Maharaja of Baroda, Sir Sayaji Rao Gaekwar allowed it to be displayed as a mark of his respect for the British sovereign. It was also the last occasion it was photographed.

The exhibition catalogue dated 1903, gives the history of the Pearl Carpet thus:

'Baroda: The Pearl Carpet — The most wonderful piece of embroidery ever known as the chaddar or veil made by Kunde Rao, the late Gaekwar of Baroda, for the tomb of Mahomed at Medina. It was composed entirely of wrought pearls and precious stones, disposed in an arabesque pattern and is said to have cost ten millions rupees. Although the richest stones were worked into it, the effect was almost harmonious. When spread out in the sun it seemed suffused with a general iridescent pearly bloom, as graceful to the eyes as were the exquisite forms of its arabesques.'

The circular portion was probably originally intended as the veil or canopy and with the rectangular carpet shown on the walls of the Loan Collection Gallery close by, is one of the four pieces that are said to have formed the carpet. According to the official report that accompanied these most curious and interesting exhibits, it is affirmed that the entire series cost Rs. 60,00,000. The field is in seed pearls, the arabesque designs in blue and red being worked out in English glass beads with medallions and rosettes of diamonds, rubies, emeralds, freely dispersed. Four large weights in solid gold, thickly set in diamonds were constructed to be placed on the four corners of the carpet. Needless to add, this superb gift never went to Mecca.

The Pearl Carpet's travels were updated in January 1994, when a news item appeared in Indian and Arabian newspapers, disguising the Baroda Pearl Carpet as a 400-year-old treasure, so that its history, barely 125 years old, could not be traced.

The Indian Prayer Rug: An ancient Islamic prayer rug,

made in India nearly 400 years ago and estimated to be worth US $ 30 million had been put up for sale in Bahrain according to a report in a Saudi Arabian newspaper. The rug, 2.75 m in length and 1.75 m in width, bursting with diamonds, pearls, gold and other precious stones, is currently on display at a museum in Hong Kong with the owner, a Saudi businessman, hoping to bring it to Saudi Arabia in search of a buyer.

The above report did not mention the name of the owner. However, it quoted a Saudi-based agent, Mr. Hisham-al-Baroodi, as saying that he was currently negotiating with relevant Saudi officials to take the rug to the kingdom, where he was confident of finding a buyer. The report described the rug as being decorated with three shining diamonds in the middle, laced with pure gold and surrounded by blue, red and turquoise-blue pearls. It was claimed to have been previously kept in a bank safe in Geneva.

The report added that transportation costs from Geneva to Hong Kong, with associated security payments, ran in excess of US $ 30,000. Legend has it, the report said, that the rug was made about 500 years ago on the orders of an Indian king.

According to eminent Bombay jewellers, this Indian national treasure has now vanished into the vaults of one of the multi-billionaire Arab oil magnates, and the outside world may not see it again.

The Parthenon and the Taj Mahal

To a vast segment of humanity, the Taj Mahal signifies the ultimate in architecture. But, if there is to be an international poll on the question, it would not be altogether surprising to note, that there is another edifice, the famous Parthenon in Greece, which may make the first prize to the Taj Mahal a disputed affair. As the oft-quoted accolade stated in Europe says, 'All the Old World's culture culminated in Greece, all Greece in Athens, all Athens in its Acropolis, all the Acropolis in the Parthenon'.

As is well known, the Taj Mahal (correctly known as Rauza-i-Mum Taj-i-Mahal or Tomb of the Most Exalted in the Palace), was built by Emperor Shah Jahan (1628-58), of the Mughal dynasty, as a memorial to his consort, Empress Mumtaz Mahal, who died in child birth in 1634. Her two last wishes were that the Emperor should build a monument of unequalled beauty in her memory and that he should not remarry. The Taj Mahal was completed in 1656 after twenty two years of labour, and has been aptly described as 'A tear drop on the cheeks of time'.

The Parthenon, the centre Temple of a group of Greek

temples known as the Acropolis, was built between 447 and 432 BC, 2,100 years before the Taj Mahal. It was erected near the Greek city of Athens and was dedicated to Pallas Athene, the patron goddess of the city. The present structure is the third temple built on the same site. Its immediate predecessor was built in 483 BC and was demolished by the Persians during their sack of the Acropolis in 480 BC.

The Greeks rebuilt it in 447 BC, with the famous engineers Ictinus and Callicrates, as the architects, and the well-known sculptor Phidias, as the supervisor. No mortar or cement has been used in the structure. All the blocks were fitted with the greatest accuracy and were secured by metal clamps or dowels, which were leaded into place. It took fifteen years to complete the Parthenon.

But in 1687, when the Venetian general, Morosini, was besieging Athens, the Parthenon was used as a gunpowder magazine and a stray cannon ball, causing an explosion, destroyed the entire central part of it.

To the Western eye, the perfection of the Parthenon is complete, whereas many eminent European architects have confessed that there is a hypnotic quality about the Taj which frightens their occidental approach to architecture.

The Parthenon is, said to represent the highest achievement of Greek architecture and reflects the rationalized ideal of the Hellenic mind. The perfection of its proportions and details, have so impressed modern architects that many attempts, frequently fantastic, have been made to define some 'infallible' rule of beauty. Professor Robert W Gardiner, for instance, is said to have discovered a formula of 'architectural beauty from the Parthenon, that dimensions must be based on sides of the squares with related areas'.

About the Parthenon it is said that the general impression it imparts is one of repose, of a sensitive balance between the supporting members and the load between the vertical line and the horizontal line, both largely unbroken. Everything contributes to calmness.

Furthermore, though this monument is simple in appearance, its simplicity is not that of ignorance. The builders of the Temple had a fine command of the language of architecture, yet gave to this building a look of simplicity.

There have been several eminent architects who have seen the Taj Mahal as well as the Parthenon and it is interesting to consider their views on the relative beauty of these two grand edifices.

Havell, the distinguished archaeologist, protests strongly against the very idea of comparing the Taj Mahal with the Parthenon. 'Should one compare Homer with Euripides?' he queries, 'or the *Mahabharata* with the *Odyssey?* The Parthenon is only a jewel box, a container for the idol of the supreme Goddess Pallas Athene, whereas the Taj Mahal is the jewel itself. It is India's Venus de Milo, the apotheosis of Indian womanhood'.

It may be that this quality of human personality is too nebulous to analyse architecturally, though it has been felt by everyone who has entered the ambience of the Taj Mahal. The Taj is a great, ideal conception that belongs to sculpture, rather than to architecture.

In the Parthenon the principle interest in this building, which is the symbol of its era and has been endowed with almost mystic significance, lies in the 'optical refinements' which its architect introduced into its design. Ictinius considered every possible aberration with which the human mind can be afflicted when examining a structure and took the trouble to make allowances for these.

In short, whereas every detail of the Parthenon has been studied, nobody has attempted to analyse the shadowy unearthliness that distinguishes the Taj Mahal from other build-

Critics agree that the Taj Mahal has been built with an effort to secure an appearance of perfect equilibrium and although the tomb is, in itself, a complete unit of design, it is effective only when seen in its setting of tropical foliage and gardens, with flanking mosques and gateways of red sandstone. By means of such contrasts, a floating, almost evanescent quality, is given to the focal point of the entire design — the Tomb.

But the Parthenon has been built without much thought to its environs. To quote Sir Edwin Lutyens: 'In construction, the Greek was not imaginative, for he never tried to roof a great space, nor was he wide minded in another respect. A map of the Acropolis shows how haphazard is the placing of buildings on the hill'.

'A regular layout is not called for on a hill of irregular shape. But some sense of order is desirable, so that the buildings may look as though grouped around and leading to the Parthenon at the summit. But actually, on the Acropolis, the buildings seem to have been dropped anywhere, like chicken houses scattered in a field. The Greeks could design

The Parthenon Today

a single building, but did not think of each building as a part of a greater whole'.

Sir Edwin Lutyens, amongst the most eminent of modern builders, was called the '20th century Wren' and served as President of the Royal Academy. Sir Lutyens reached Athens with great expectations of seeing the Parthenon. He even had a special glass made so that he could view the great temples in their pristine glory. But he was sorely disappointed. The barren grayness of the Acropolis was a great shock, as was the Parthenon's casual, undramatic setting and pathetic ruin.

'Was this uninspiring, literally blasted fragment, the epitome of architecture?' he mused. 'The most tragic spot I ever visited', he said to his wife, 'heart breaking to see the utter valuelessness of human endeavours. The Parthenon was there, all I knew it to be ... but oh ... so little of it. No one silhouette was perfect, the restorations being attempted woeful ... It is a glorious remnant of what has never at its best been a unit perfect in itself. The craftsmanship, the cutting of the marble was superb. But the work is not so convincing, when it comes to the bonding of external angles of their cellars'.

'The Parthenon has no relation to its site, no dramatic sense such as the Romans had. The site must have been chosen by extraneous causes, like the setting of an eagle, or a prophet's dream'. Later, he told architectural students in Britain that while seeing the Parthenon, he was conscious only of tragic waste, but that even so, no one could say that it was dull.

The Taj Mahal, however, moved Lutyens. Not as architecture, but as science. He described to Lady Hardinge, the occasion when he had visited Agra and seen the Taj Mahal four times within twenty four hours, under four different conditions, ... by rain, by sun, by moon and after a hail and thunderstorm.

'Hail lay about and all the ponds and pools and grass spaces were deep in water. The golden leaves, blown about and all clean and sweet, made a wonderful picture. The great white clouds were reflected in the water and were made to appear as deep as the sky was high. But by moonlight, the moment when romantic tourists were most agreeably affected, he noticed that it all became blurred and indefinite. The patterns disappeared and the arch forms merged into a fog of white reflections.'

It is another critic, James Fergusson (*History of Indian and Eastern Architecture* Vol. II), who actually comes to grips with the problem of evaluating the Taj Mahal and the Parthenon and one cannot do better than quote him. 'The Taj Mahal and the Parthenon', he writes, 'are buildings nearly equal in size and magnificence, both in white marble, admirably adopted for the purpose for which they were built. But they have nothing in common'.

'The Parthenon is simple in its outline and depending on pillars for its external adornment; the other has no pillars and owes its greatest efforts to its singularly varied outline and the mode in which its various parts are disposed, many of them wholly detached from the principal mass'.

'The Parthenon belongs, as it is, to a higher class of art, its sculptures raising it into the region of the most intellectual branch of phonetic art: but on the other hand, the exquisite inlay of precious stones at the Taj Mahal is so aesthetically beautiful as in a merely architecturally estimate almost to bring it on a level with the Grecian masterpiece'.

'Though their value may consequently be nearly the same, their forms are so essentially different that they hardly look like "productions of the same art" and in an art so essentially conventional as architecture always is and must be, it requires long familiarity with any new form and a knowledge of its origin and use, that can only be acquired by constant study'.

Adopting the numerical scale described in the introduction to the *True Principles of Beauty in Art (History of Ancient and Medieval Architecture* Vol.1), Fergusson estimated the Parthenon as possessing 4 parts of technic value, 4 of aesthetic, and 4 phonetic or 24 as its index number. The Taj Mahal, on the contrary, he estimated as possessing 4 technic, 5 aesthetic, and 2 phonetic, not that it has any direct phonetic mode of utterance, but from the singular and pathetic distinctness with which every part of it gives utterance to the sorrow and affection it was erected to express. Its index number consequently is 20.

But to Eastern eyes, the Parthenon does not evoke any upsurge of feelings, like the haunting refrain and undercurrent of grief that the Taj Mahal brings to the viewer.

Mahatma Gandhi's Gift to Queen Elizabeth

One of the treasures in the vaults of the British royal family is a cotton shawl — Mahatma Gandhi's gift to Queen Elizabeth II, on her marriage to Prince Philip on November 20, 1947. Thereby hangs a human interest tale which throws light on the 'home spun' simplicity of the Mahatma and the respect the Queen gave to this valued gift. In fact, this cotton shawl figured as the last item on display during the famous 'Exhibition on the Raj' held in London's National Portrait Gallery in March 1991, as a symbol of the friendship which Great Britain and India have shared since Indian independence in 1947, after 200 years of British domination of India.

In November 1947, Lord Mountbatten was preparing to visit London for the marriage of his nephew, Prince Philip with Princess Elizabeth. The Indian Cabinet decided that the elder statesman, C. Rajagopalachari (Rajaji), should officiate as Governor General during Mountbatten's absence. But who could be deputed for Lady Mountbatten for her numerous 'Mercy Missions' co-ordinating refugee relief? She herself felt that, despite her close relationship to the British royal family, it would be 'leaving the post of duty' during India's hour of crisis. As she was mulling over what to do, Mr. Nehru, the Indian Prime Minister, told her that he would ask the Mahatma to try persuading her to attend the marriage of the future Queen. Mahatma Gandhi accordingly visited the Viceregal palace (Rashtrapati Bhavan) on Nehru's suggestion and advised Lady Mountbatten to attend the function as she would be representing the people of India by her visit. She ultimately agreed and his task completed, the Mahatma prepared to depart. Earlier when Lord Mountbatten had mentioned the royal wedding to the Mahatma, the latter in accordance with his generous nature had expressed a desire to send a wedding gift to the young couple. After much deliberation, the Mahatma who had no worldly possessions to send decided on a shawl. As he was taking his leave of the Mountbattens, he (to quote the writer Robert Lacey), 'shyly drew something wrapped in tissue paper from the folds of his shawl'.

'I had a special reason of my own for coming to see you', he told the Governor General and his wife, 'I know that you are taking an official wedding present with you from the Government of India. (A rare antique Rajasthani diamond necklace.) But I have brought a very small gift of my own for the Princess and your nephew.'

He handed over the package to Mountbatten, who opened the tissue-wrapped packet to reveal a shawl. 'This little thing is made of doubled yarn of my own spinning. The knitting was done by a Punjabi girl. Please give the bride and bridegroom this with my blessings, with the wish that they would have a long and happy life of service to humanity'. Lord Mountbatten promised to hand it over personally to the couple in London. Later, while handing over the gift to the young Princess, he told her that this was the most precious wedding gift she had received.

The marriage, scheduled for November 20, 1947,

attracted gifts from all over the world. They ranged from priceless diamond jewellery sent by the Indian Maharajas, to clothing coupons from British housewives, given as a mark of their affection (it was barely two years since the end of the Second World War). Fifteen hundred of the most valuable presents were displayed for public viewing and as more and more gifts poured in, the British royal family would occasionally take the time to view them. The most valuable of the lot was the priceless rose tinted diamond necklace given by the Nizam of Hyderabad from India. From within the royal family itself, the finest gift was the pearl jewellery given by Queen Elizabeth (the present Queen Mother), to her daughter.

As for the Mahatma's gift, well, the Countess of Airlie, a Lady-in-Waiting to Queen Mary (wife of King George V and grandmother to the present Queen), says that as the royal party came to the table where the shawl was displayed, the Queen Mother became very angry to see the yellowish piece of handwoven cloth. She exclaimed, 'What is this loin cloth doing here? What does Gandhi mean by presenting this ... this is an insult!' Initially, none of the royal party dared to contradict the grande dame. But Prince Philip, the bridegroom, boldly disagreed with her saying, 'I do not agree. Mr. Gandhi is a very great man.' But the Queen frostily moved on. The next day, as the royal party headed by her visited the display again, Princess Margaret decided not to chance another outburst from the former Empress of India. Darting ahead of the party, she took the 'loin cloth' and hid it behind another present so that the Queen Mother would not see it.

But Queen Elizabeth has no such allergy towards the gift. The priceless diamond necklace given by the Nizam of Hyderabad, is no longer an individual piece in her collection, having been used to make up a tiara some years ago. But even decades after her marriage, when some newspaper reporters questioned her about the whereabouts of the shawl, the Queen (one of the richest women in the world), knew the exact location of the Mahatma's gift among her innumerable treasures.

Fabulous Thrones of India

The end of the fabulous era of the Maharajas marked the final phase of the democratization of Indian society. A throne may be an anachronism in a republic, but in bygone eras, it signified power and the thrones of Indian royalty had the rich patina of history.

At the same time, it is to be regretted that sufficient care has not been taken by the Government of India to ensure that the vast array of State Regalia, especially the thrones of over five hundred former Indian princes, are given the status of National Treasures. Incidentally, during their days of suzerainty in India, the British never allowed the Indian princes to use the word 'throne' for the regal chairs from which they ruled. Only the Indo-Persian word of *Gaddi*, which meant the 'noble seat', was permitted, as in British-Indian protocol, only the King of Great Britain (who was also the Emperor of India), had the right to use the words 'throne' and 'royal'. Further, by subduing in conquest Indian sovereigns like Maharaja Duleep Singh of the Punjab and Tipu Sultan of Mysore, the British ensured that the fabulous thrones of these opponents were taken to Great Britain as war spoils.

Traditional Gaddi or Masnad (Throne) of the Kota Maharaja

Of all Indian thrones, the most famous has been the Peacock Throne of the Mughal Emperors, fabricated out of 1150 kg of gold and 230 kg of precious stones. After his victory over the Mughals in 1739, Nadir Shah, the Persian Emperor, took away this throne to his country and the throne was destroyed during the internecine wars that ravaged Persia after his death in 1747. It is thought that parts of the original Peacock Throne were used to form the throne on which the last Shah of Iran was coronated. Another famous throne of Indian history was the Tiger Throne of Tipu Sultan (1749-99), named for the two snarling tigers at its pedestal.

James Forbes in his book, *Oriental Memoirs Vol. II*, writes, 'Tipu Sultan's proud boast was that he would rather live two days as a tiger than two hundred years as a sheep. He adopted as the emblem of his state and as a species of armorial bearings, the figure of the royal tiger, whose head and stripes constituted the chief ornaments of his throne and of almost every article which belonged to him. This throne was of considerable beauty and magnificence. The support was a wooden tiger as large as life, covered with gold, in the attitude of standing. His head and forelegs appeared in front

Throne of Tipu Sultan. Inset: *Tigerhead Finial of Tipu's Throne*

and under the throne, which was placed across his back. It was composed of an octagonal frame, eight ft by five ft, surrounded by a low railing, on which were ten small tiger heads of gold, beautifully inlaid with precious stones. The ascent to the throne was by small silver steps on each side. From the centre of the back part, opposite the large tiger's head, arose a gilded iron pillar, seven ft high, surrounded by a canopy, superbly decorated with a fringe of pearls. The whole was made of wood, covered with a thin sheet of the purest gold, richly illuminated with tiger stripes and Arabic verses. The Huma bird, Persian symbol of prosperity, was placed at the top of the canopy and seemed to flutter over the Sultan's head. This bird, the most beautiful and magnificent ornament of the throne, was sent by the Marquis of Wellesley, the Governor General of India, to the Court of Directors. It was about the size and shape of a pigeon and intended to represent the fabulous bird of antiquity, well-known to all Persian scholars, a bird peculiar to the East, supposed to fly constantly in the air and never to touch the ground. It is looked upon as a bird of happy omen and that every head it overshades will in time wear a crown. The tail of the Huma bird on Tipu's throne, its wings, were in the attitude of flying. It was formed of gold, entirely covered with diamonds, rubies and emeralds.'

This fabulous throne was destroyed by the British Army Prize Agents in 1798, after the defeat of Tipu Sultan, so that the gold sheets covering the throne could be distributed as prize money to the British Army. Few portions of this famous throne, including two of the tiger-face supports, are kept in the Powys Castle Museum in Great Britain. A few years after the destruction of the throne, a British artist drew from memory a picture of the throne, with the gold Huma bird. Decades later, Prince Ghulam Muhammad (son of Tipu Sultan), visiting Great Britain, confirmed that the real throne was more or less as depicted in the picture.

Another famous throne taken away by the British, the throne of Maharaja Ranjit Singh, the last independent ruler of the Punjab, is kept today at the Victoria and Albert Museum in London.

To quote historian Khushwant Singh: 'In the correspondence on record is a letter dated December 19, 1850, from Lord Dalhousie to the Directors of the East India Company, asking whether they would be interested in acquiring the golden chair in which the *burra* Maharaja (Ranjit Singh) held his Court'. Apparently they were, and later gifted the throne to Queen Victoria.

Throne of Maharaja Ranjit Singh

The ultimate resting place of the throne of the great warrior-king, Shivaji, continues to intrigue historians. A few years ago, extensive searches were made by the Central Archaelogical Department of the Government of India, at the Raigarh Fort in the state of Maharashtra, where Shivaji was crowned Chhatrapati (Independent King), free of Mughal suzerainty in 1674. Local legends aver that this famous throne weighing nearly 80 kg and encrusted with jewels, was thrown into the tank inside the Raigarh Fort, to prevent the Mughal forces (who captured Shivaji's son, Shambaji) from taking it away. Despite pumping out the 50 ft deep tank, the Archaeological Department was unable to find the throne.

Of the famous thrones still extant in India, the top place goes to the throne of the Pandavas (the heroes of the *Mahabharata*), now in the Palace-Museum at Mysore. Another historian refers to it as the historic throne of the Indian Emperor Vikramaditya (after whom the Hindu Era is named), lost for centuries and later rediscovered from an obscure cave by the equally famous Emperor Bhoja. After the death of this legendary monarch, the throne was lost to history.

In the 16th century AD, with the rise of the Vijayanagar Empire in South India, Guru Vidyaranya, the preceptor of the royal family, found this throne and used it as the coronation chair of the Vijayanagar kings. The Vijayanagar Empire came to an end in 1565, and this throne passed on to the Mysore maharajas in 1609. Another historian refers to it as the gift of Emperor Aurangzeb in the late 17th century, to the Kings of Mysore!

When the adventurer, Hyder Ali took over the reins of Mysore state 150 years later, he did not wish to use this throne with its Hindu pantheon representations. Following the defeat of Hyder Ali's famous son, Tipu Sultan, the British discovered this throne in the lumber rooms of the palace at Srirangapatnam. For the last two centuries, this has been the coronation throne of the maharajas of Mysore. Made of fig wood, it was originally covered with ivory. Later, this ivory casing was replaced with gold and silver panels, emblazoned with Hindu mythological figures.

Surprisingly, the throne of the Nizam of Hyderabad, the richest of the Indian princes, is a simple affair, carved out of plain white marble. Kept in an austere Durbar Hall in the Chowmohallah Palace at Hyderabad, it has yellow cushions and at each corner of the throne platform are clusters of yellow chandeliers shaped akin to the mitre-like headdress of the Nizams.

Travancore State in south India is famous for its ivory thrones. A number of exquisitely carved ivory thrones were presented by the maharajas of Travancore to the British Crown and are now in the royal collection. The famous Indologist, Stella Kramrisch, found a 200-year-old ivory throne in the Rangavilasam Palace in Trivandrum and describes it as covered with ivory slabs with exquisite designs carved into them, as if in filigree. Due to the ravages of time, the ivory has begun to contract, creating gaps in the throne.

The British who ruled India for almost two hundred years, never brought their coronation thrones to the subcontinent. But, during the Delhi Durbar of 1911, a costly and serious problem faced the Government of India — the necessity of providing a royal throne for the Emperor of India for the grand ceremony. It was suggested that the most economical course would be to cast a silver throne out of the silver reserves held in the Government of India Mint and to restore the silver by remelting the throne after the Durbar. It was felt that if a throne was made in the open market, a good deal of the cost could be recovered by selling it. But on paper, the cost of buying the throne would appear enormous and when the time came, it would be regarded as sacrilegious to sell a throne, which had been used for such a grand ceremonial purpose ... finally, a bright official decided that the ideal plan would be to allow the Mint to make the throne — the metal being classed simply as, 'Held in Reserve'. Nobody would then be able to object to the subsequent remelting of the throne.

The Finance Minister of the Government of India found the proposal to be most ingenious and ordered that the nine tons of silver lying idle in the Mint, could be used and if more was required, it could be taken temporarily from the stock of withdrawn and non-current coin. The only reservation he expressed was that the silver throne would not be restored to the Mint and might be gifted away to the Victoria Memorial at Calcutta, then being built as a Museum for British achievements in India.

The Viceroy promised to help in preventing this historical throne from being gifted away to the Victoria Memorial and the work began in real earnest, the famous Calcutta jeweller's firm of Hamilton & Co., being asked to cast the throne. Strangely enough, it was only at this stage that it was realised that actually two thrones had to be made as there was an Empress of India to be accommodated.

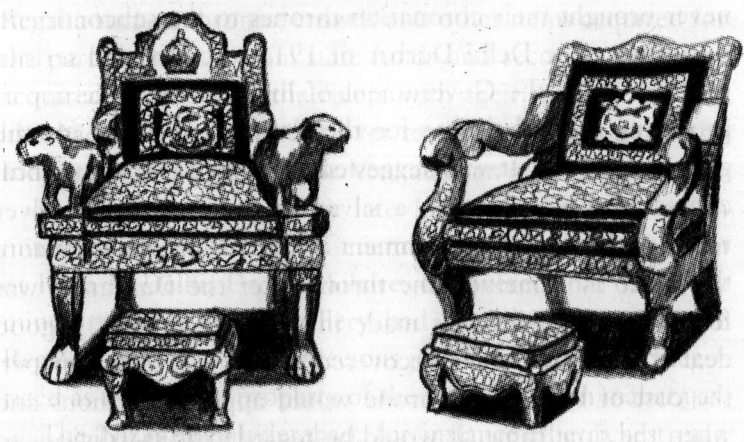

Silver Thrones of the Delhi Durbar (1911)

The final designs as approved, called for two thrones of solid silver 'gilded' all over. The Emperor's throne was to weigh 510 kg and the Empress's 360 kg. But in those halcyon days, the total cost of the two thrones was only Rs. 82,500. Today, the silver content alone would cost Rs. 7,000,000. Six new cushions were to be made for the thrones and pads for the footstools, upholstered in best quality silk, velvet and gold embroidered, with English gold bullion fringes. These cost Rs. 1,750. Today, the same upholstery would cost over half a million rupees.

In order to accommodate the heavy thrones, the Delhi Durbar Committee was ordered to ensure extra heavy platforms for the Durbar Hall to prevent accidents. After the Durbar, the thrones were kept for a long time in the Viceregal Palace at Simla for safe custody, as the thrones had been created out of Indian revenue. It would have been 'wrong' to take the regal chairs out of India, and the Viceroy, a mere representative of the Emperor and his wife, could not be allowed to sit on the same thrones. At this juncture, news leaked out in Government circles that after the Durbar the thrones would be melted down. Many British people were desirous of possessing the historic thrones and offers came from interested parties. Some maharajas offered to buy the thrones as well. But the Government of India opined that as they had been used for the coronation of the Emperor of India, it was in the highest degree improbable that the Government would entertain any proposal for the sale of these thrones. In 1963, after the former Viceregal Palace in Simla was given to the Education Department of the Government of India, to house an Institute of Humanities, these thrones were removed to the Government of India Mint and later to the museum of Rashtrapati Bhavan in New Delhi. Strangely enough, the same upright code of behaviour did not apply to the special crowns made for the royal couple out of

Indian revenues. These were blithely taken back to Great Britain as State Regalia.

The Viceroy and the Vicereine had their own thrones to preside over State occasions in India. The Emperor's thrones, as well as the Viceregal chairs, are now kept in the special museum attached to Rashtrapati Bhavan in New Delhi. Many smaller thrones owned by the former Indian princes have been melted down by them in order to secrete away the gold and silver. In this way priceless specimens of the Indian jewellers' art, have been lost forever.

A few years ago, with their 'owners' running short of cash, the thrones of the former rulers of Nayagarh and Ranpore were advertised for sale in Orissa. Fortunately, the state government bought the treasures for Rs. 25,000 and thus preserved them for posterity.

Mahatma Gandhi, Einstein and the Atom Bomb

What did Mahatma Gandhi, the crusader for non-violence, think of the atom bomb? How desperately did Einstein, the 'Father of the atom bomb', want the Mahatma's help to fight this bane that science had released on the world? Now, five decades after the deaths of prominent statesmen and scientists of that era, the archives of many international institutions are available for our reference and throw interesting side lights on Mahatma Gandhi, Einstein and the atom bomb.

In the words of the Mahatma, 'I did not move a muscle when I first heard that the atom bomb had wiped out Hiroshima. On the contrary, I said to myself, "unless now the world adopts non-violence, it will spell certain suicide for mankind" '.

It is interesting to consider the various aspects of the bomb vs non-violence discussion that found reflection in the innumerable queries placed before Gandhiji by critics, followers and just plain friends, from all corners of the world.

One British correspondent told him that the use of the atom bomb had brought victory to the Allies. The Mahatma replied 'The atom bomb brought an empty victory to Allied arms, but it resulted for the time being in destroying the soul of Japan. What has happened to the soul of the destroying nation is yet too early to see.' One journalist wanted to know from the Mahatma how a small nation could defend itself against an adversary using the atom bomb. The Mahatma answered: 'However small a nation or even a group may be, it is able, even as the individual is able, to resist the atom bomb, provided that it has the mind, will and the guts to defend its honour and self-respect against the whole world in arms. Therein consists the matchless strength and beauty of the unarmed. That is non-violent defence, which knows not nor expects defeat at any stage. Therefore, a nation or a group which has made non-violence its final policy cannot be subjected to slavery, even by the atom bomb'.

It is not so well known to the world that Mahatma Gandhi had decided to make the outlawing of the atom bomb one of the missions of his life. This he had promised to Jawaharlal Nehru, his political-spiritual heir and the first Prime Minister of independent India. In Nehru's words: 'When I heard of the bombing of Hiroshima and Nagasaki, I was badly shaken. Soon after this awesome development, I went to see the Mahatma and spoke to him about the horrors of the atom bomb. He put to me many questions about the atom bomb, its making, its capacity to kill and the horror it created in the Japanese city. There was a look of revelation about his eyes, as he stared into unplumbed depths. After listening to me silently with deep human compassion in his gentle eyes, the Mahatma told me that this wanton destruction had confirmed his faith in God and non-violence and that now he realised the full significance of the holy mission and divine purpose for which God created him and armed him with the sacred weapon of non-violence'.

But less than three years after the first nuclear explosion, even the Mahatma fell a victim to violence in 1948. Mankind had turned a blind eye to his teachings.

Within two years of the death of the Mahatma, Nehru had the opportunity to meet Professor Einstein in US and told him about the Mahatma's unfulfilled desire to devote himself to the banning of the atom bomb. Einstein was delighted and told Nehru: 'It was Gandhi's mission. And as his disciple you should take over the task ...' Nehru felt that Einstein was deeply disturbed about the fact that it was his discovery of the Relativity Theory that led to the creating of the atom bomb and wished, in some way, to atone for it. He told Nehru that he had always felt that the Mahatma's commitment to the principle of non-violence closely paralleled the development of the atom bomb.

In Nehru's own words: 'Einstein spoke to me with great emotion ... The Mahatma's technique of a bloodless struggle successfully waged, represented to Einstein the only possible answer to the riddle of life and death, universal prosperity and total annihilation posed by this nuclear era to human civilisations. After that, I remember he took a pad and pencil and wrote down a number of dates or years on one side and events on the other, to show the parallel evolution of the nuclear bomb and the Mahatma's non-violent struggle, respectively, almost from decade to decade since the beginning of this century'.

It seems an extraordinary coincidence really how these two contradictory phenomenon, the non-violent crusades and the all destructive atom bomb developed in an almost exact parallel. I cannot recall the exact dates and incidents now, but it seems that when Einstein and other scientists were working in Europe on the formula that made the splitting of the atom possible, during the first decade of the century, the Mahatma was conducting his first experiment in peaceful non-violent protest in South Africa, up till the 1940s when his non-violent 'Quit India' struggle against the British coincided with the American atom bomb project. Finally, of course, came Hiroshima and Nagasaki in 1945. About the same date, according to Einstein, the Mahatma's doctrine of peaceful non-cooperation had tamed the might of the world's greatest empire and negotiations for the British withdrawal from India had started. Einstein paid Indian freedom its finest compliment of proving the superior strength of non-violence over imperial violence.

The 'Lost' Bible

The earliest copies of the Bible, with the exception of the Dead Sea Scrolls, are the *Codex Vaticanus* at the Vatican Library and the *Codex Siniaticus* at the British Museum. But the Anglican Church obtained in the 19th century, copies of the Bible, supposed to be as old as the copies at the Vatican and in London. These Indian national treasures are now at the Cambridge University in UK and it is interesting to consider the dramatic history of these thousand-year-old antique copies of the Bible from India.

The earliest bibles were in Aramaic, Hebrew and Greek and early in the fifth century AD St. Jerome translated the entire Bible into Latin from the original languages. This version of the Bible, known as the Vulgate Bible, forms the main authoritative version used by the Roman Catholic Church.

Another branch of Christianity had established itself at Antioch in Syria and its version of the Bible had been taken to Malabar in India, as Indian Christianity dates from the first century AD, following the arrival of St. Thomas, one of the twelve apostles of Christ in AD 52. The Archbishops of the Malabar Church had been nominated by the Patriarch (Head of the Eastern Orthodox Church) from Antioch and the

Syrian Christian liturgy of Malabar forms one of the most ancient liturgies in the world. The Syrian version of the Bible differs in many ways from the Roman Catholic version and is considered to be the original Bible, as it is supposed to have been brought to India before AD 325, the year when the Christian Council at Nice, decided to codify the Bible according to the Roman Catholic version. The Indian Christian community in Malabar, however, continued to follow the Syrian version.

In 1498, the Portuguese came to India and brought with them the tenets of the Roman Catholic Church. While they were happy to find an indigenous Christian community in Malabar, the Portuguese were determined to remove the influence of the Patriarch of Antioch from the Indian Church and wished the Indian Christians to transfer their allegiance to the Pope in Rome. This caused frequent strife between the Portuguese and the Indian Christian community in Malabar.

Finally, in 1599 AD, Archbishop Menezes of Goa, as the representative of the Pope in India, decided that the main cause of the obstinacy of the Indian Christians was their version of the Bible, with its differences from the Roman Catholic version. He felt that this 'Syrian Bible' ought to be destroyed.

Employing methods of intimidation and cajolery, along with demonstrations of armed might, he compelled the Syrian Christian clergy of India to bring all their theological literature to Udayamperoor (known to the Portuguese as Diamper), in Malabar. There he convened a Synod, the purpose of which was to remove 'errors' from the Syrian bible. At this Synod, which lasted for a week, all Syrian manuscripts which did not agree with the Roman Catholic version of the Bible were burned together with other documents that would have sustained the Syrian Christians in their differing beliefs. At one stroke, the Portuguese obliterated all manuscripts and documents relating to Syrian Indian

Christianity prior to 1599 AD. Further, the complete library of the Syrian Archbishop at Angamale was destroyed. These acts of literary ruination have been considered by historians to be vandalism comparable to the burning of the Great library of Alexandria by Caliph Omar in AD 643.

The Syrian Indian clergy had not suspected such vandalistic intent by the Portuguese and it was too late for their shocked leaders to rescue any of the theological books. But providentially, the Portuguese Archbishop's message to bring the theological volumes to Udayamperoor, had not reached one of the remote mountain churches of central Malabar and one copy of the Syrian version of the Bible escaped destruction. Later, this copy became the most treasured volume of the Syrian Church in India and a veil of secrecy surrounded this Bible, which was 'lost', its whereabouts known only to a very few at the topmost echelons of the Syrian Church.

Two centuries later the British missionary Dr. Claude Buchanan came to Malabar and was very much interested in the history of the Syrian Christians. The interest shown by Dr. Buchanan in their way of life, won for him the friendship of Mar Dionysius, the Head of the Syrian Christian Church, and in 1807, he told Dr. Buchanan about the existence of the 'lost' Bible. To quote Dr. Buchanan, 'The volume contained the Old and New Testaments embossed in strong veleum in large folios, having three columns to a page and was written with beautiful accuracy. The characters were of Estrangelo Syriac and the words of every book are numbered. But the volume has suffered injury from time and neglect. In certain pages, the ink has been totally obliterated from the page, leaving the paper in its natural whiteness, but the letters can in general be distinctly traced from the impress of the pen or from the partial corrosion of the ink.'

Dr. Buchanan discussed with the Archbishop Mar

Dionysius the brittle condition of the volume and told him that in case the book was entrusted to him, he would have it printed and thus preserved for posterity. The Archbishop thus faced a very difficult decision, for this volume had been preserved for over a thousand years.

At the same time, he knew that the British were fast becoming masters of India and that they, compared to the Portuguese, were more broadminded as to religious convictions. More importantly, the Archbishop was unsure how many more years they themselves would be able to preserve the 'lost' Bible. Scarcely a decade earlier, the destruction of Indian Churches by Tipu Sultan had erased many a landmark and even the famous Mission at Verapoly had lost all its manuscripts, as the boat carrying the treasures sank in deep water. The Archbishop felt that once printed and thus preserved, this ancient version would be safe forever and so gave the manuscript volume to Dr. Buchanan. Dr. Buchanan gifted these 'thousand-year-old volumes' and many other Syrian manuscripts, to the Cambridge University, where they are still preserved at the University Library.

In 1815, this ancient Bible was printed by the British and Foreign Bible Society. Christian theologians have found to their pleasant surprise, that this Syrian version was free of many of the 'later insertions' that are prevalent in the modern Bible and thus it was proved to be a valuable reference volume.

For India, it is a matter of great pride, that the country which is the home of major religions — Hinduism, Islam, Christianity, Buddhism, Jainism and Sikhism and the last refuge of Zorastrianism — was also the country where such rare copies of the Bible were successfully preserved for centuries, even before Europe accepted Christianity. The history of this 'lost' Bible is an illuminating one, which reveals that India safeguarded Biblical manuscripts, even from fanatical Christians like the Portuguese.

The English East India Company

February 13, 1601, is a memorable date in Indo-British relations, for, nearly four centuries ago, on this day, the English East India Company's first fleet of four ships started on their epic voyage to the East and the subsequent founding of the greatest empire in history. Nine years earlier, the accidental capture of a huge Portuguese galleon trading with the East, had revealed to the English the lucrative nature of the trade and on December 31, 1600, the last day of the 16th century, Queen Elizabeth I issued to a body of 125 merchants in London, a Royal Charter constituting them as the 'English East India Company'. The original investment was £72,000 and according to the Charter, only six ships and six pinnaces were allowed to be plied in the Eastern trade.

In this first expedition, the Commander of the fleet, Captain Lancaster, took with him a letter from Queen Elizabeth I to Emperor Akbar, whom she addressed as 'The Most Invincible and Mightie Prince, Lord Zelabdin Echebar, King of Cambaya'. But the primary voyage was mainly to the spice islands of what is now modern Indonesia and only in 1608, did one of the East India Company ships touch Surat, on the western coast of India.

Originally Queen Elizabeth I had granted the monopoly for a period of 15 years, but her successor King James I, erased the word 'limitations' and extended the concession for ever. The Royal Charter prescribed 24 Directors to form the Board and one Governor, to act as the Chairman. The trading capital was raised by subscriptions from amongst the various members for various voyages or stocks, which were wound up after the particular voyage had concluded and the vessel returned from the East.

Coat of Arms, English East India Company

The number of votes held by each member was denoted in the official register by asterisks placed against the name. According to the law passed in 1773, the possession of £1000 worth of shares gave one vote, although persons having only £500 worth of shares were allowed to be present at the Court of the Board of Directors. Shares for £2000 gave two votes, for £6000 three votes and for £10,000 four votes. In 1843, fifteen years prior to the dissolution of the Company, there were 2003 share holders, out of whom 44 had four votes each, 64 had three votes, 333 had two votes and the rest one vote each.

Incidentally, the English East India Company was only one

amongst the numerous East India Companies formed in Europe for trading with India. In the 17th century, more than 15 companies were formed in England, Holland, France, Denmark, Scotland, Spain, Austria and Sweden, with the intention of trading with the East. But with the exception of the English, French and the Dutch concerns, none of them prospered.

The English East India Company's advancement was slow as far as political advantages were concerned. It was only in 1606, seven years after the formation of the Company, that its envoy John Hawkins, finally gained audience with the Mughal Emperor Jahangir, to secure permission for the establishment of a factory in India and in December 1612, the first English factory was built in Surat. In 1639, Fort St. George was built in Madras and in 1668, the Fort was erected in Bombay, to be followed 22 years later, by the purchase of three villages near modern Calcutta to house factories. But by 1680, the East India Company began to rule the residents inside the forts and the nuclei of the three Presidencies of Bombay, Madras and Bengal were formed.

The Company's real bid for political power started and succeeded on June 23, 1757, when at the battlefield of Plassey, the Company's forces under Clive defeated Siraj-ud-Daula, the Nawab of Bengal. More than the territorial gains, the huge amounts collected as war reparations, stabilized the Company's finances — between 1757 and 1766, the princes and commoners of Bengal had to pay £60,00,000 as compensation to the East India Company.

But the Company had not yet come into conflict with the forces of the Grand Mughal at Delhi, who was still the titular ruler of India. It was the victory at the Battle of Buxar in 1764, when the Company forced the Mughal Emperor to cede to it the revenues of the royal provinces of Bengal, Bihar and Orissa in return for a payment of £3,00,000 which made the Company the supreme political factor in the Indian subcontinent.

However, the position of the Company with the British Government at home was not a comfortable one. From its inception in 1600 to the 1750s, it often had to loan huge amounts running into millions of pounds, either to the King or the British Government, so as to safeguard its monopoly of the Indian trade. In fact, in 1657, the Board of Directors of the East India Company tired of it, threatened the British Government that if it was further pressed for loans, the Company would sell all its factories, privileges and would not hesitate to abandon its trade with India.

For a time the British Government refrained from further demands, but later, when another group of merchants offered £20,00,000 as loan, in return for permission to start a rival East India Company, it readily agreed to the request. It then required all the influence of the old East India Company to buy off the shares floated in the new Company, and in 1709, both the Companies merged into one.

According to a parliamentary return cited in Chandler's *History of the Proceedings of the House of Commons*, the dividends of the East India Company, from 1657 to 1691, amounted to no less than 840 per cent on the original paid up stock. This included a record dividend in January 1682, when upon the arrival of eight ships with cargoes valued at half a million pounds, a dividend was ordered at 150 per cent, of which a third was to be distributed in cash and the remainder paid for the uncalled portions of each member's share. In 1740, the capital was £3,000,000 and the dividend was at seven per cent. The usual imports from India consisted of pepper, tea, coffee, spices, silk, cotton goods, ebony, fine woods and export to India was mainly metals like iron, lead and so on.

According to the historian Tucker, the wealth the East

India Company obtained from India every year, besides the above mentioned transactions, could be classified as follows: public tribute of upto £40,00,000 per annum; private fortunes which went out of India at the rate of £30,00,000 per year. A deficiency in India's annual exports was present, so that a remittance by means of her produce and manufacture was needed. This amounted to £30,00,000 to 40,00,000 per annum. In all, it formed a total of £11,000,000 or fifteen crores of rupees.

Until the 1780s, the Company was able to show sizeable profits in its dealings. But once the Company encroached into Indian politics and began to take up responsibilities for the internal administration of the country, it was reduced to the verge of bankruptcy. The Company was unable to keep up its payments, amounting to £400,000 per annum, to the British Government, and these ceased completely in 1770. This state of affairs could not be allowed to continue and in 1773, the Company was forced to ask for a loan of £1,000,000 from the British Government. The Government agreed to extend a loan of £1,040,000 at four per cent interest and further granted the monopoly of shipping tea to America. In return, all the territory acquired by the Company to date and in the future, was to be Crown property. The Directors of the Company were well aware that the commerce they carried on now in India, could not flourish without the fostering care of a paternal Government. Its struggle with Indian powers like Tipu Sultan, the Marathas and the Sikhs, received the full backing of the Government and the show went on till the Sepoy Mutiny of 1857 destroyed the Company.

Economically, the East India Company had proved to be a cancer on the Indian economy and many well established industries like ship building and textiles were ruthlessly destroyed so that English goods would have an open market in India. The Company carried a public debt of £10,000,000 in 1792, and by 1857, the struggle for power in India had increased it to over £59,000,000. Further more, after the failure of the Mutiny, by the India Act of 1858, the British Government paid £12,000,000 to the East India Company as compensation for taking over the Indian Empire and debited the amount to the Indian Public Debt Act. Within sixty-five years, the East India Company had saddled India with a public debt of over £70,000,000, where none existed before, and further, this amount was exclusive of the £98,000,000, the debts of the East India Company (including £37,000,000 for suppressing the Mutiny), which was charged to the Indian Treasury.

Against this total, the British investment in the East India Company and for 'safeguarding India', was £1,30,000,000 in 1858. Three-fifths of the public debt of £70 000,000 belonged to Englishmen and an additional £10,000,000 was invested in India. A sum of £80,000,000 was invested in the East India Company's shares, stocks, deposits, debentures, loans and the Indian Railways, making a total of £130,000,000.

But what does the modern Indian intellectual think of the East India Company and its successor, the British Government in India? Here one cannot do better than quote the late K.M. Munshi, one of the pillars of modern Indian thought and culture, 'It is true that the British sapped India of its economic resources. But to achieve that purpose it had to provide an efficient administration. The British also produced the dominant minority of English educated Indians. Hankering for many things, which were inconceivable to the older generations, this minority created the modern Indian Renaissance. Among them was the desire to break the age-old isolation of the country, to modernize its static social institutions, to recreate the strength and vigour of its languages, to transform its hide-bound intellectual and religious outlook and above all, to accept the challenge of the West and generate the strength and power to secure the country from political subjugation. Finally, India was won over to the English judicial system, which awakened the urge to vindicate just rights.'

But, that the vast Empire which had grown up in the East should be administered by the British through a body, which was nominally a commercial concern, had long been an anachronism, and slowly the British Parliament began to remove the main props of the Company. The monopoly over the Indian trade was finally withdrawn in 1813, and in 1833, the tea trade with China was removed from the preserves of the Company.

Historians have advanced many reasons for the outbreak of the Sepoy Mutiny that made the dissolution of the Company imperative. Among the significant ones was the Doctrine of Lapse, initiated by Lord Dalhousie, the Governor General of India in the 1850s. According to the Doctrine, the Governor General was entitled to take over the administration of those Indian States whose rulers died without leaving natural heirs. On many occasions the Governor General decided against the adopted heirs, the most famous instances involving the Peshwas of Poona and the Rajas of Jhansi. These Company Acts made the Indian princes apprehensive about their future and an anxious British Government found that in quelling the Mutiny, they must end the Company also.

The Company, founded under Queen Elizabeth I, had been remodelled under Queen Anne and now it was to be wound up under Queen Victoria. Its doom was pronounced in 1858, just over 250 years after the first ship reached the coast of India and a little more than a century after the Battle of Plassey, which laid the foundations of its territorial powers.

In February 1858, the Company presented a petition to Queen Victoria, in a final attempt to safeguard its existence

Queen Victoria in 1877

and offered to allow a Minister of the Crown total control of the administration of Indian affairs, assisted by a Council of eighteen Directors of the East India Company. But the Sepoy Mutiny, which occurred at a time when the Company was maintaining a force of 238,000 troops in India, made the British nation alert and the Prime Minister advised the Queen to reject the petition.

The powers and duties of the East India Company were now transferred by an Act of the British Parliament to a new Secretary of State for India, who was to be assisted by a Council, somewhat analogous to the old Court of Directors, and partially recruited from them. The Company itself was not abolished, indeed, it could not be, for under the Act of 1833, the share holders were guaranteed an annuity of £630,000 for a minimum period of forty years. But the East India Company was reduced to a skeleton, with a Chairman, five Directors, a secretary and a clerk. The Company's offices were situated first in Moorgate Street and then in Pancras Lane, in London.

In this condition, it continued till the time arrived when the right of redemption could be exercised. On March 15, 1873, an Act was passed which enabled the Secretary of State for India, in Council, to give the stock holders the option of taking Indian stock in lieu of their holding or of being paid off at the stipulated rate. At the same time, it was enacted, that on the completion of this final operation, the East India Company, now a 'shadow of the shade', should be dissolved and dissolved it was, on June 1, 1874.

The Costliest Treasure in History

The fabulous Peacock Throne of the Mughals, cost twice as much as the Taj Mahal and was crafted for the same Emperor, Shah Jahan (1628-58). Zille-i-Ilahi or Shadow of God on Earth, was one of his titles. As befitted the title, Shah Jahan, the fifth emperor of the dynasty, created in his palaces at Agra and Delhi, the 'Shadow of Paradise on Earth', and in his throne, sought to re-create the 'Shadow of the Throne of God' on earth, taking for a model, the famous throne of Solomon, the prophet-king.

One thousand one hundred and fifty kg of gold and 230 kg of diamonds, rubies, emeralds, sapphires, pearls and other precious stones, were used in its making. It took the craftsmen of the Imperial Treasury seven years (1628-35), to complete the work under the supervision of master jeweller Bebadal Khan, and it formed the costliest single treasure in history.

One cannot do better than quote the contemporary eye witness, Mughal court chronicler, Nizam-ud-din Bakshi, who wrote in 1635, 'In the course of years many valuable gems had come into the Imperial Jewel House, each one of which might serve as an eardrop for Venus or could adorn the girdle of the Sun. Upon the accession of Emperor Shah Jahan in 1628, it occurred to his mind that, in the opinion of farseeing men, the acquisition of such rare jewels and the keeping of such wonderful brilliants can only render one service — that of adorning the throne of the Empire. They ought, therefore, to be put to such use that beholders might share and benefit by their splendour, and that, his Majesty might shine with increased brilliancy. It was accordingly ordered that, in addition to the jewels in the Imperial Jewel House, rubies, garnets, diamonds, rich pearls and emeralds, in all weighing 230 kg, should be brought for the inspection of the Emperor and they should be handed over to Bebadal Khan, the Superintendent of the Goldsmith's department. There was also to be given to him 1150 kg of pure gold ... The throne was to be three yards in length, two and half in breadth and five in height and was to be set with the abovementioned jewels. The outside of the canopy was to be of enamel work with occasional gems, the inside was to be thickly set with rubies, garnets and other jewels and it was to be supported by twelve emerald columns. On the top of each pillar there were to be two peacocks, thick set with gems and between each two peacocks, a tree set with rubies and diamonds, emeralds and pearls. The ascent was to consist of three steps set with jewels of fine water'.

Of the eleven jewelled recesses formed around it for cushions, the middle one was intended for the seat of the Emperor. Among the historical diamonds decorating it were the famous, Kohinoor (186 carats), the Akbar Shah (95 carats), the Shah (88.7 carats), the Jehangir (83 carats) and the second largest ruby in the world — the Timur ruby (283 carats). A twenty couplet poem by the Mughal poet-laureate Qudsi, praising the Emperor in emerald letters, was 'embedded' in the throne.

Conservatively, the throne would in 1995 have cost

US $ 804,000,000 or Rs. 25,728,000,000. On March 12, 1635, Emperor Shah Jahan ascended for the first time the newly completed Peacock Throne in the imperial fortress at Agra. The French jeweller-cum-traveller, Jean Baptiste Tavernier, who had the opportunity to examine the throne at close quarters, confirms the court chronicler's description. The doyen among historians of the Mughal era — Sir Jadu Nath Sarkar states: 'The Peacock Throne consisted of a gold plated frame capable of being taken to pieces, richly jewelled panels fitting into its eight sides and detachable pillars, steps and roof. It used to be put together and placed in the ceremonial halls only at the anniversary of the royal coronation, but at other times, it was stowed away in loose parts its place in the two fortress-palaces of Delhi and Agra was usually at the Hall of Private Audience known as Diwan-i-Khas, although it was kept at the Hall of Public Audience known as the Diwan-i-Am when larger audiences were expected.'

Emperor Shah Jahan's son, Aurangzeb, usurped the throne in 1658, ruled for forty-nine years and died in 1707. By then, the Mughal rule in India had become weak and in 1739, the Persian Emperor Nadir Shah overran the Mughal Empire, defeating Emperor Muhammad Shah. He looted Delhi, carrying away the Peacock Throne to Persia, along with other treasures valued (at today's prices) at US $ 50 million or Rs. 1800. In 1747, when Nadir Shah went on a campaign against the Kurdish tribesmen, he was assassinated by his own officers. In the ensuing melee the costliest treasure in history, the Peacock Throne, was demolished by the tribesmen and the jewels taken away to hideouts all over the Middle East. Although some Persian historians mention the Peacock Throne even two decades later, it is known that only a few pieces of this fabulous throne were rescued, later to be incorporated in the Persian Nadiri Peacock Throne, kept in the Gulestan Palace in Teheran today. Bereft of the Peacock

Throne, the Mughal Emperors built for themselves an imitation Peacock Throne and later found it difficult to maintain even this fake throne. When the British captured the Red Fort-palace complex in 1857, during the Sepoy Mutiny, the last Mughal Emperor, Bahadur Shah, had only a Peacock Throne covered with silver sheets. Many miniatures showing the throne or copies of the original miniatures, exist in Indian, European and American art museums. But the controversy over why only four pillars are shown in many of the thrones, has caused eminent historians to doubt whether any authentic picture of the original Peacock Throne exists today. In this context, the eminent historian of Mughal India, Abdul Aziz (1884-1970), opined that for a complete view of how the original Peacock Throne appeared, we have to refer to the miniature (that of Emperor Akbar Shah) of the imitation throne, made after Nadir Shah took the original away in 1739. In recent times, it was discovered that the *Padishahnama*, a picture album showing the court life of Emperor Shah Jahan, acquired by the British royal family in the 1790s, has a miniature showing the original twelve pillared throne partially.

Excerpted from the book "The Peacock Thrones of the World" a reference anthology by K.R.N. Swamy and Ms. Meera Ravi, ISBN 81-85796-00-9.

The Mahatma's Encounters with British Statesmen

Despite the fact that he was 'weaving a shroud for the British Empire in India', Mahatma Gandhi never harboured any animosity against the British and this was apparent to many eminent British statesmen from the very first instance they came into contact with him. But to these 'pillars of the British Empire', it also appeared on many occasions, that the Mahatma was a shrewd politician in the guise of a saint. This may have been due to the fact that whenever they met the Indian leader, they were aware that his objectives were political, namely, the ending of British rule in India.

The Mahatma himself realized that his motives were suspect to British statesmen. It has been said of Gandhi that he 'was often driven to the verge of despair by the wall of prejudice behind which British statesmen entrenched themselves. When he criticised their actions he was denounced as a demagogue; when he claimed to be their friend, he was accused of hypocrisy; when he applied for an interview he was suspected of outmanoeuvring the Government; when he circumscribed the scope of his revolt and withdrew it, he was alleged to have lost credit with his followers'.

Of all the British leaders, His Majesty's Prime Ministers was the one to whom the saint-politicians's policies caused the maximum trouble. Lloyd George, for instance, felt that the Mahatma's assertions did not appear to be straightforward. In 1931, the former British Prime Minister met Gandhi at Harley College in UK and had an illuminating talk with him. According to Lloyd George, Gandhi was present with bare legs and sandals, but swathed in a heavy blanket like a bath robe, for it was raining. The Indian leader and the British statesman talked for hours and Lloyd George stated that Gandhi did most of the talking.

The Mahatma told him that he was willing to have India under the umbrella of the British Commonwealth of Free Nations. Lloyd George was not convinced of this and queried, 'Have you said so in a public speech?' and told the Mahatma that he had not heard of this 'important statement'. The Indian leader agreed that if necessary he would make a public statement regarding his views. Lloyd George later pithily remarked, 'Gandhi may be a saint ... but he is also a very shrewd politician ... he wants the best of both worlds'.

Another British Prime Minister, Winston Churchill, had met the Indian leader in 1908, as the then Under Secretary of State for Colonies. The Mahatma (then plain Mr. Gandhi), had come to London leading the Transvaal Indian delegation to plead the cause of Indians affected by the anti-Asiatic legislation in South Africa. According to the Mahatma, 'We met Mr. Winston Churchill at the time fixed by him. He spoke nicely and promised to do all he can if the delegates can send him a report.'

But twenty-three years later, when the Mahatma came to London in 1931 for the Round Table Conference, Winston

Churchill was not willing to meet him. The Mahatma learned that the British leader could not see him and had fulminated earlier against a 'half-naked fakir' climbing the steps of the Viceregal Palace at Delhi to parley on equal terms with the Viceroy. In London, at a meeting held at Guild Hall, somebody asked him about this remark made by Churchill. The Mahatma jocularly replied, 'I shall have to admit that as long as I have a body, I must wrap it with something. But, if anyone wants to take it off me, I shan't call the police.'

Later in 1942, it was during Churchill's Prime Ministership that the Mahatma was imprisoned and there were many eminent Commonwealth statesmen who felt that Churchill was treating the Indian leader with vindictive anger. One of them was the late Field Marshal Smuts. Lord Moran in his memoirs mentions that in August 1942, Churchill met Smuts at Cairo, while the British Prime Minister was on his way to meet Stalin in Moscow. The Mahatma was in prison and during dinner, Smuts told Churchill, 'Gandhi is a man of God. You and I are mundane people. Gandhi has appealed to religious motives. You never have. That is where you have failed.' Churchill laughed and told Smuts sarcastically, 'I have made more bishops than anyone since St. Augustine.'

Apart from the British Prime Minister, the Secretary of State for India was the minister primarily responsible for dealing with the Indian Empire and it is interesting to learn the views of three such eminent statesmen, about the Mahatma. Edwin Montague, said on November 26, 1917, that, 'Gandhi is a social reformer, he has a real desire to find grievances and cure them, not for any reasons of self-advertisement, but to improve the conditions of his fellow men. All he wants is that we should get India on our side. He wants the millions of Indians to leap to the assistance of the British Throne.'

But fourteen years later, the Mahatma had become a

visionary, crusading for Indian freedom and in 1931 in London, the then Secretary of State Sir Samuel Hoare (the future Lord Templewood), states that he looked forward to the meeting with some trepiditions. 'It was a very cold autumn afternoon, when my magnificent Royal Marine messenger showed him into the Secretary of State's room in the India Office. He was in his habitual *khaddar* and looked even smaller and more bent than his pictures had shown him. His sharp penetrating eyes seemed to take immediate possession of the whole room at a glance. His bony knees and toothless mouth would have made him ridiculous, if they had not been completely overshadowed by the dominating impression of a great personality.'

The Secretary of State continues, 'As I spoke, I remembered Dostoevsky's description of the visit of the Karamazov family to Stantetry Xosima and the ignominous result of their attempts to hide their motives from a very astute holy man. I was determined not to make the same mistake. Gandhi at once responded to my approach. He was obviously relieved that there was to be no make-believe between us ... The result was a series of very frank discussions between us and the start of a friendship, shown by many letters, all of them written in a beautiful flowing hand, that continued till his tragic death.'

Lord Pethick Lawrence, who as the Secretary of State for India saw the Mahatma's dream of a free India become reality, had many points in common with him. Lord Pethick Lawrence and his wife's prominent roles in the suffragette movement had brought him and the Indian leader together. In a BBC broadcast in 1954, the former Secretary of State for India said that the Mahatma reminded him of John the Baptist, and added, 'Even when we disagreed, I never doubted his sincerity or single-mindedness nor he mine. It was not easy to conduct negotiations with Gandhi, owing to the subtlety of his mind, which makes it impossible to assess at their true value, the precise meaning of the words'.

But, the task of preventing the Mahatma from weaving a shroud for the British Empire in India rested ultimately with the Viceroy in India and the Governors of different provinces and nobody envied them their jobs. In fact, there was a rumour that those British personnel holding high administrative ranks in India were instructed to avoid meeting the Mahatma lest they fall under his spell. Lord Reading who had seven meetings with the saint-politician, wrote to his son how affected he had been by the Mahatma's personality when he began to speak, 'He is direct, there is no hesitation about him and there is a ring of sincerity in all he utters. He expresses himself well in excellent English, with a fine appreciation of the value of words he uses'.

Of all the Viceroys he had dealings with, it is said that the Mahatma had the greatest rapport with Lord Irwin, the Viceroy of India in 1930. It was mainly due to this Viceroy's efforts that Gandhi participated in the Round Table Conference of 1931. Lord Irwin wrote to King George V as follows, 'I think that most of the people meeting him would be conscious, as I was conscious, of a powerful personality and you cannot help feeling the force of character behind the sharp little eyes ... he affirms, that although his aim is that of Purna Swaraj (complete independence), India will be still requiring British help. I believe it Sir, to be definitely untrue to suggest, as I see it suggested from time to time, that he is out to break the unity of Your Majesty's Empire'.

Years later, Lord Irwin (then Lord Halifax), one of the most successful British diplomats, confessed, 'There was a directness about him, which was singularly winning. But this could be accompanied by a subtlety of intellectual process, which could sometimes be disconcerting. To appreciate, what was passing in his mind, it was necessary, if not to start from the same point, at least to understand, very clearly what was the starting point for him and this was nearly always very human and very simple'.

The next Viceroy was Lord Willingdon, the only Viceroy who did not see the Mahatma during his role as the leader of the Indian freedom movement. Lord Willingdon, had a deep ill-conceived prejudice about the Mahatma and was convinced that the only way to deal with him was to keep him at arm's length and be firm. He would never meet him because (the Viceroy thought) that the Mahatma was so subtle in argument that he could 'tie you up in knots'.

The next representative of the British Crown, Lord Linlithgow, tried to avoid meeting with the Mahatma on one pretext or the other. In fact, it took him more than a year to make up his mind to see the saint-politician. By then the World War II made any constructive decisions impossible.

With the next viceroy, Lord Wavell, the position was even more difficult. To Lord Wavell, a blunt soldier, the Mahatma, a lawyer, was an irksome 'juggler of words'. Referring to one of their meetings, Lord Wavell said that the Mahatma spoke to him for half an hour and 'I am not sure as to what he meant to tell me ... Every sentence he spoke could be interpreted at least in two different ways ... I would be happier, were I convinced that he knew what he was saying himself. But I cannot even be sure of that'.

Finally, the very prospect of another talk with the Mahatma began to cause the Viceroy so much mental discomfort that he became sleepless the previous night and in the words of one of his aides, 'The Viceroy would sit there, while the little man prattled on and the expression on Wavell's face was one of sheer misery. He would fiddle with his pencil and I could see his single eye gradually beginning to glaze and at the end of it, all he could think of to say would be "I see ... thank you"'.

The crisis came on August 27, 1946, when the Viceroy lost control of himself during a meeting with Gandhi and Nehru and shouted at Nehru during a particularly tense period, 'For God's sake, man! Who are you to talk of blackmail?' To the Mahatma, this was a signal that the Viceroy was losing his mental balance and returning to his camp, the Indian leader sent a cable to British Prime Minister Attlee, expressing concern at the Viceroy's state of mind and opined that Lord Wavell was becoming unnerved by the communal holocaust going on in Bengal, and the Mahatma wanted the British Prime Minister to bolster the Viceroy with an abler 'legal mind'. To Lord Wavell himself, the Mahatma did not mince words and wrote the same day, 'Several times last evening you said that you were a plain man and that you did not know law. We are all plain men although we may not all be soldiers and even though some of us may know law'.

With other factors, this telegram from the Mahatma who was the key figure in Indian politics, had its effect and Lord Wavell was shortly afterwards replaced.

The next Viceroy, Lord Mountbatten, although a soldier, was of a different mould. When the Viceroy's invitation arrived, the Mahatma was in Bihar, on a pilgrimage of penance 'to quell the communal strife'. He replied to the Crown Representative, 'Although I have difficulty in moving out of Bihar's riot torn villages, I dare not resist your kind call'.

Lord Mountbatten was determined to make a success of this first meeting with the saint-politician and was prepared to talk with him for hours, without any agenda. On the first day the Mahatma talked almost for three hours mainly about his early life and struggle. The next day, the Mahatma told the Viceroy that he had no objections if he handed over power to the Muslim League (headed by the founder of Pakistan — Mr. Jinnah), the arch rival of the Indian National Congress, in the interest of communal peace.

The Viceroy knew that this idealistic solution would not work and that the pragmatic leaders of the Congress Party like Nehru and Patel, would not concur with the Mahatma's suggestion. The Viceroy politely agreed to discuss the suggestion of the Mahatma and decided to do business on more practical lines with the political parties, with a plan to partition India.

Still, Lord Mountbatten did not underrate the Mahatma's influence and when the Indian leader came to see him after expressing opposition to the partition idea, the Viceroy knew that this was going to be the most crucial moment of his assignment.

But 'the little man in loin cloth' also knew that the Viceroy had won the game. He knew that his desire for an independent, undivided India would not bear fruit mainly due to the strength the Viceroy derived from the Mahatma's disciples, Nehru and Patel, for his partition plan and that India was going to be divided.

Therefore, when the meeting (so much dreaded by the Viceroy) took place, Mahatma Gandhi wrote on a scrap of paper that it was his day of silence, he had nothing to say and added, 'You do not really want me to say anything ... do you?'

The Viceroy of India, Lord Mountbatten of Burma, the former Allied Commander-in-Chief of South East Asia during World War II, the hero of many battles, breathed freely and knew that he had won the greatest victory of his life.

How They Met the Mahatma

When, after a day's hard work in the Courts, a busy lawyer goes to the Club for a quiet game of bridge, he can be forgiven if he becomes annoyed at finding the card tables deserted and the members gone for a public meeting. That was what Sardar

Nehru, Gandhi & Patel

Vallabhbhai Patel, a brilliant lawyer of Ahmedabad, encountered when he went to the Ahmedabad Club one evening in 1916.

An enquiry revealed that the meeting was being held in the central hall of the Club and that the speaker was a fellow-Gujarati who had recently returned from South Africa. Mr. Patel had heard about this speaker, who had the reputation of having made a ruthless South African Government relent. From sheer curiosity he went to the main hall to listen to the speech. At first he was sceptical that the frail figure in an outsize turban on the platform was indeed the fabulous 'giant-killer'.

Still, as he listened to the soft voice explaining the problems of Indians in South Africa, Mr. Patel felt strangely drawn towards the man. He who came to scoff, remained to pray. Sardar Vallabhbhai Patel had met the Master — Mohandas Karamchand Gandhi.

It was not in an aristocratic club of an Indian city, but in war torn Britain that Sarojini Naidu, the eminent poetess-stateswomen first saw the man whom she later called, 'Father of the Nation'. She was in London in 1914 and World War I had just begun. A committee of Indian ladies had been formed to make bandages for use on the battlefield and Mrs. Naidu was a volunteer. She had heard that M.K. Gandhi, the famous South African Indian leader, was arriving in Britain by ship that day and that he had experience of this kind of work, having organised an ambulance corps during the Zulu Wars of the 1890s.

Unfortunately, she was unable to meet the ship when it arrived and the next day, August 8, 1914, she trudged in search of his lodgings in a suburb of London. Finally she located the house.

To quote her own words, she found 'an open door framing a living picture of a little man, with shaven head, sitting on the floor on a black prison blanket and eating a messy meal of squashed tomatoes and olive oil — out of a wooden bowl. Around him were ranged battered tins of parched ground nuts and tasteless biscuits of dried plantain flour.'

Unable to control herself Mrs. Naidu burst into peals of laughter. Mahatma Gandhi lifted his eyes and also laughed, saying, 'Ah! You must be Mrs. Naidu. Who else dare be so irreverent? Come in and share my meal.'

Mrs. Naidu's heart missed a beat at the very idea of having to share the 'food'. 'No thank you', she replied, making a wry face. 'What an abominable mess it is ...' and became his disciple unto the last.

The young Asaf Ali, one of the pillars of the freedom movement in India, first heard the Mahatma speak in 1909. It was during a Dusserah function held in a London restaurant. Used as he was to the fiery declamations and perorations of Vinayaka Damodara Savarkar and leaders like Bepin Chandra Pal, on India's right to freedom, the almost inaudible voice of this simple lawyer was a refreshing change.

But alas, for a person of the eminence of the late Aga Khan the plain words of the Mahatma did not seem so. Writing about their first meeting, the Aga Khan says Mahatma Gandhi and he had corresponded with each other since 1899, when both of them were interested in the South African Indian problem, although they did not meet till 1931.

The Mahatma had gone to London for the Round Table Conference and went to see the Aga Khan at the Ritz Hotel. Mrs. Naidu accompanied the Mahatma, and press photographers, ever alert for such a strange combination of 'asceticity and princely wealth', requested them to pose for a photograph.

The trio obliged and then withdrew to the Aga Khan's suite for the meeting. The very first topic was inevitably, Hindu-Muslim Unity. In a patronising tone, the Aga Khan said that if Gandhi showed, at this juncture, a 'paternal' affection for the Muslims, the Hindu-Muslim problem would be solved in no time. The Mahatma looked at him and remarked, 'I can never take a paternal attitude towards the Muslims... there is no place for sentiment now and the agreement has to be of a political nature.'

In the words of the Aga Khan, this remark threw a 'cold douche' on the talks and their effect was to pervade and contaminate the later proceedings. Years later, the Aga Khan mentioned this episode to the Mahatma and the saint-politician was shocked to hear about this misunderstanding. 'I very well remember the occasion', replied Gandhi, 'BUT YOU ARE VERY, VERY, VERY, much mistaken. What I meant was that I can never take a superior paternal attitude towards the Muslims and that I can consider them only as blood brothers, my equals.' (The capitalization of letters are the Mahatma's.)

To an undergraduate, Vinobha Bhave (later the saintly leader of the Indian Bhoodan Movement of the 1950s, when millions of acres were gifted to landless labourers by rich landlords), who had left his classes in Poona to join the Mahatma's Ashram in 1916, the leader was plain spoken. The Master and the disciple came down to earth, brooded over the matter together and decided that Vinobha should return to college to complete his Sanskrit studies.

Vinobha Bhave went back for a year of academic studies and then returned, punctual to the day. 'I had forgotten that he was to return that day,' remarked Gandhi, marvelling at the steadfastness of the disciple and till he died in the late 1970s the disciple strode in the footsteps of the Master.

But in the case of Madelaine Slade (Mira Behn), the daughter of an Admiral of the Royal Navy, there had to be more planning. She expressed, in a letter to the Mahatma, her desire to join the Ashram and share the purity of the life there. In 1925, she left the luxury of her home in London for a hut in Sabarmati Ashram.

She arrived in Sabarmati, escorted by Mahadev Desai, who had gone to the railway station to receive her. She found it difficult to control her emotions as the Mahatma accepted her obeisance and told her, 'From now on you are my daughter'.

In her turn, a princess of Kapurthala, Rajkumari Amrit Kaur, had to wait for some time to join Gandhi's camp, although she had met him as early as 1910. Gopala Krishna Gokhale, who was a family friend, used to tell her about the Mahatma. Even her father, Raja Harnam Singh, said, 'One day I hope you will see the man destined to do great things for India.' The day came during the Bombay session of the Indian National Congress in 1915, when Amrit Kaur pledged allegiance to him and his way of life.

For a daughter of multi-millionaire lawyer Pandit Motilal Nehru, next only to the Mahatma in the Indian National Congress in the 1920s, there was no question of joining the Ashram, for the residence of the Nehrus (which gave independent India three successive Prime Ministers) was itself a political camp. Arriving at the Bombay residence of Motilal Nehru, the Mahatma was welcomed by the great lawyer and his beautiful nineteen-year old daughter Vijayalakshmi (later, as Mrs. Pandit she was to be the first woman President of the United Nations General Assembly), saw Gandhi for the first time.

But there was no time for small talk, as the infamous Rowlatt Act curbing public meetings was soon to be passed. The discussions dragged on till dinner time and the Nehrus, who dined in Western style, 'relaxed' the rules and spread a mat on the floor for the Mahatma. It was then that the impulsive Vijayalakshmi asked the Mahatma, 'Why shall we not fight the British?' and the apostle of non-violence had to explain his policy. Little did the young lady realise that one day she would enter the Court of St. James as the accredited

Indian High Commissioner to the United Kingdom.

Acrimony began rearing its ugly head when the Mahatma met Muhammad Ali Jinnah, the founder of Pakistan, for the first time. In 1916, there was a political conference at Godhra in Gujarat and among the speakers were Gandhi and Jinnah.

The future Mahatma insisted that the speeches be made in Gujarati by the Gujarati-speaking delegates. Jinnah, whose fluency in his mother-tongue of Gujarati was limited, objected to the suggestion, but finally agreed to it. 'Gentlemen, I am speaking today in Gujarati as ordered by Mr. Gandhi. Having made the first part of my speech in Gujarati, I will complete it in English,' said the Muslim leader and went on to finish the speech in English. In a way this action was symbolic of his life, for he began his political career as an ardent supporter of the Gandhian ideal of Hindu-Muslim unity and later drifted to become the creator of the Islamic State of Pakistan.

Even in those days, the Shantiniketan Academy of the acclaimed poet Rabindranath Tagore, was free from political bickering and Gandhi visited it in 1915, to see the poet. Tagore had earlier welcomed a few members of the Mahatma's Phoenix settlement in South Africa to Shantiniketan, when that centre was disbanded. The Mahatma was anxious to see them and thank their benefactor, Tagore. On February 17, 1915, he arrived at Shantiniketan and an enthusiastic crowd welcomed him with traditional honours. But Tagore was away in Calcutta and Gandhi returned once again on March 10. He was given an affectionate welcome by Tagore and even today, March 10 every year is celebrated in Shantiniketan as Gandhi Day, when all the menial staff are given a holiday.

But the welcome he received in the house of the future first President of India, Dr. Rajendra Prasad, when Gandhi went there for the first time, was quite the opposite of the welcome he had received in Tagore's abode. Rajendra Prasad had gone to Puri for some work and Raj Kumar Shukla, who had brought Gandhi to inquire about the plight of indigo plantation (British owned) workers at Champaran in Bihar, took him to Rajendra Prasad's house.

The servants, who were unaware of the identity of the honoured guest, treated him the way they would an ordinary man. In caste-ridden Bihar no exceptions were made and the Mahatma was not allowed into the inner precincts of the house. Even his bath had to be taken outside. Gandhi then shifted to the house of a Muslim friend. A few days later Mahatma met Rajendra Prasad and the future disciple felt abashed on being introduced to the Mahatma. He had been to his house and had heard about the treatment the Mahatma was given there. But the Master just laughed and remarked, 'I have been to your house'.

Down south in Madras, in 1919, his experience was much more strange. He did not know whose guest he was, though he stayed in C. Rajagopalachari's (the first and only Indian Governor General of the Dominion of India from 1948-50) house for two days. Gandhi had gone to Madras at the invitation of the famous journalist, Kasturi Ranga Iyengar, and he was under the impression that he was that gentleman's guest. Later, Mahadev Desai, the Mahatma's secretary, informed him who his host in fact was, and the Master was rather diffident about meeting such a shy host. Finally, Mahadev Desai brought C. Rajgopalachari to him and into Gandhian politics. In fact, C.R.'s daughter Lakshmi, later married the Mahatma's son, Devadas Gandhi.

The Mahatma himself punctiliously observed the laws of hospitality and when in 1915, Professor J.B. Kripalani (one of the future Presidents of the Indian National Congress) visited him in Shantiniketan, he insisted on Kripalani being his guest and not Tagore's, as Kripalani had come to see him.

Strangely enough, his meeting with his 'heir-apparent',

Jawaharlal Nehru, during the Lucknow session of the Indian National Congress in 1916, was most laconic.

In 1920, Gandhi met at Hakim Ajmal Khan's residence in Delhi, a 31-year old Muslim savant, by the name of Maulana Abul Kalam Azad. In Azad's own words, 'I had no difficulty in agreeing with him in every detail and later we went to Meerut to attend the Khilafat Conference'.

The Mahatma himself was eager to meet the great men of the day. Sir Phirozshah Mehta, Lokamanya Tilak and Gokhale impressed him as the Himalayas, the Indian Ocean and the Ganges respectively.

Ironically enough, ill luck dogged his attempts to see the legendary figures of Maharishi Devendranath Tagore, father of the poet Tagore, and Swami Vivekananda, the greatest reformer Hinduism has known in the modern Era.

In December 1901, Gandhi went to the residence of Devendranath Tagore to see him. He was told that no interview was possible and was instead invited to join the Brahmo Samaj function that was being held there. Thus baffled, the Mahatma went to Belur Math to see Swami Vivekananda. There he was told that the great Swami was lying seriously ill at his Calcutta residence. Perhaps it was ordained that the saint was not to see the seer.

1914: When German Warship *Emden* planned to liberate Indian Patriots from the Andamans

In the first decades of the 20th century, the Bay of Bengal (fringed by parts of the British Empire — Ceylon, India, Burma and present Malaysia/Singapore), was virtually a 'British lake'. The outbreak of the First World War in 1914 did cause a stir. However, the British did not expect, with their superior navy commanding the seas, any attacks on their Indian Empire. But, within a few weeks of the beginning of the war, the intrepid German light cruiser, *Emden*, under Captain Karl von Muller, destroyed this illusion. From August 13, 1914, for a period of three months, the *Emden* ranged 30,000 miles within the Indian Ocean/Bay of Bengal, attacking Madras harbour and other British naval/radio installations in the eastern seas; sinking or capturing 23 merchant ships, one battle cruiser and a destroyer; inflicting more than rupees twenty crores worth of damage (when a gram of pure gold could be brought for less than two rupees). All this havoc was caused despite a combined Allied naval fleet of 80 vessels (including 14 major warships) searching for the *Emden*, aided by the recently developed radio communication system.

More noteworthy was the fact, that Captain Muller brought to his task such 'chivalry, daring and humaneness', that even his sworn enemies, the British, applauded the *Emden's* victories, as if it were a cricket match. For us in India, the *Emden's* main historical impact lies in its two daring battle plans. The first was to attack the major British-Indian harbour of Madras (which succeeded). The second plan, more dramatic than the first but aborted at the last minute, was the proposed German Commando attack on the infamous Cellular Jail at Andamans to rescue the 1500 Indian revolutionaries imprisoned there and land them on the Orissa coast of eastern India, to resume their fight against the British.

As a part of the German East Asian Naval squadron, Captain Muller convinced the German Admiralty, that he would be able to sink many ships of the Allied merchant fleet in the Indian Ocean, causing the Allies to divert major naval vessels to pursue the *Emden*. This, in turn, would make it easy for the German Navy to harass the Allied ship movement in the Atlantic. As camouflage, Muller disguised the outlines of the *Emden* by adding a fourth dummy funnel to the usual three funnel configuration of German light cruisers. As British light cruisers were of the four funnel type, many of the *Emden's* victims mistook the German raider for a British warship and discovered too late, that they were at the mercy of German guns. The only problem was that of fuel (the *Emden* was a coal burning ship). It had a maximum range of 6000 miles with a full load of coal. But fortune favours the brave and the *Emden*, during her 30,000 miles swath of destruction, captured sufficient coal ships to continue her raids.

By September 15, 1914, the *Emden* had sunk 10 Allied ships and was in the vicinity of Calcutta, lying in wait for cargo ships coming out of the harbour. It was at this stage that Captain Muller decided to go down the coast to attack the Madras harbour, so that the British, unchallenged for over a century in the Indian Ocean, would suffer a rude shock. The Madras harbour had only a 30-year-old battery of 5.9 inch guns to protect it and one of the *Emden*'s crew knew the landmarks of the harbour, having worked in Madras during the pre-war years. Closing in on Madras, Captain Muller was surprised to find that the Madras lighthouse, perched on the central dome of the Madras High Court, was fully lit, despite the war, unlike other lighthouses in other British-held harbours. It was a mark of British confidence that nobody would attack them in India.

The *Emden* came as near as 3,000 m from the shore and fired 125 salvoes at the Madras lighthouse, the Burma Oil Company petroleum tanks and other landmarks in the city. Two of the petroleum tanks were set ablaze and the shore guns could barely reply with nine salvoes, only three of the shots coming within a hundred metres of the German raider. One of the shots from the *Emden* had almost hit the Madras lighthouse, demolishing one of the compound walls surrounding it. Today, a plaque on the damaged wall, commemorates the 'visit' of the *Emden* to Madras. There are a number of Madras citizens who remember the day when the *Emden* shelled the 'City of Temples'.

Its job to scare the British done, the *Emden* cruised down the coast. It was lucky to escape two pursuing warships of the Allied Naval Fleet (more powerful than the Emden), the British heavy cruiser HMS *Hampshire* and the Japanese

1914: The German Warship Emden

cruiser *Chikitama* (Japan was on the Allied side in World War I). The maps showed later, that with incredible luck, the *Emden* had actually passed between its pursuers on its cruise past the French Indian port of Pondicherry (no ships being in port, Pondicherry was not attacked), to Colombo. But by then the news of the attack on Madras had travelled fast and Captain Muller found (unlike the Madras lighthouse), the Colombo lighthouse had been switched off and searchlights were stabbing the sea in front of the harbour, watching out for the raider.

The *Emden* skirted round the coast, and went up to the Laccadivian island of Minicoy, where it captured and sank the cargo ship *Troilus*, after the customary warnings. In the Captain's cabin of the Troilus, the *Emden*'s boarding party found a consignment of Indian newspapers. What they read in the newspapers gladdened Captain Muller and his crew. The whole of India was shocked and scared by the audacious attack on Madras. The British were worried that the 'native' trust in British invincibility was shaken, and the word 'Emden' in Tamil had become a byword for courage.

German Light Cruiser 'Emden'

In Britain, Winston Churchill, as the First Lord of the Admiralty, expressed his dismay at the attack and ordered the Royal Navy to sink the raider at any cost ... the British had been humbled.

But Captain Muller had one more intrepid task to perform. Years earlier, the German Consul at Calcutta, Dr. Lendl, had visited the Andaman Islands as a 'tourist' and had noted the explosive political nature of this 'Bastille of India'. He had suggested to the German Government that if a commando raid could be organized on the Cellular Jail of the Andamans and the 1500 Indian nationalist prisoners taken away to be landed on the Indian coast near Orissa, it would shake the very foundations of British rule in India. Now, when the whole of India was agog with the revealed weakness of the British, there could be no better raider for the task than the invincible *Emden*. Captain Muller had been briefed earlier and the raid on the Andamans was scheduled for October 2, 1914.

But the raid was not to be. With dozens of Allied naval units, some of them more powerful than the *Emden*, on his heels, Muller was delayed in keeping his rendezvous with the Andamans and on October 7, 1914, the German Admiralty ordered Captain Muller to abandon the commando raid. Pragmatic to the core, Captain Muller agreed and bowed out of what would have been a thrilling chapter in India's freedom struggle.

But his masterly scheme of sinking Allied shipping and wrecking British radio navigation/communication stations in the Indian Ocean islands continued. The humane manner Captain Muller treated his victims endeared him to friend and foe alike. Finally, on November 8, 1914, the *Emden*, outgunned and disabled by the more powerful Australian heavy cruiser *HMAS Sydney*, was scuttled by Captain Muller by running it aground on the Indian Ocean island of Cocos. Ever the conservative *Times*, the foremost newspaper of Great Britain, paid eloquent tribute to the *Emden*. It is said that in the inter-war years (1919-39), a Calcutta firm removed the derelict *Emden* from Cocos island to Calcutta, for sale as scrap iron. But no proof exists as to this mundane end of the famous ship. However the *Emden* and its chivalrous Captain live on in the annals of Indian history as a symbol of an 'audacious gracious era in War'.

A British Viceroy's Tribute to a Mughal Empress

Two hundred years of overlordship in India saw many famous British people come to the subcontinent to serve as proconsuls of their Sovereign. They ranged from the ardent cattle-lover, Lord Linlithgow to Lord Minto, who once in a parsimonious mood, proposed to demolish the Taj Mahal and sell the marble. Fortunately for the world, the contractors advised him that the cost of demolishing the Taj Mahal would be more than the sale value of the marble and thus the mausoleum escaped destruction.

Among such a galaxy, the name of Lord Curzon nevertheless stands out prominently. Even now, nearly nine decades after he left the shores of India, he remains a highly controversial figure.

But one thing is certain, lovers of Indian architecture owe a debt of gratitude to this Viceroy, who did more to preserve Indian heritage from the ravages of time, than any other occupant of the Viceroy's august post. When Curzon arrived

Lord Curzon

in India, the total amount spent per annum on the preservation of ancient monuments was £7,000. In 1904, following Lord Curzon's stewardship of India, it rose to £37,000 and in the city of Agra itself, over £50,000 was spent during his Viceroyalty.

Of all the Indian archaeological marvels, he had the greatest regard for the Taj Mahal and he spared no effort to ensure that the mausoleum remained always in its pristine glory. 'The Taj is incomparable', he wrote to his friend John Broderick, describing his feelings on seeing it for the first time, 'designed like a palace and finished like a jewel, a snow white emanation starting from a bed of cypresses and backed by a turquoise sky, pure perfect and unutterably lovely. One feels the same sensation as in gazing at a beautiful woman, one who has that mixture of loveliness and sadness which is essential to highest beauty.'

During one of his many visits to Agra, he made a catalogue of the items that had been removed from the Taj Mahal in the decades of political unrest that followed the fall of the Mughal Empire. Of them all, the item whose disappearance he regretted most, was that of a gold chandelier, that used to hang above the cenotaph of the Lady of the Taj, Empress Mumtaz Mahal.

This chandelier had been removed by the Jats, during their occupation of Agra in the 17th century and Lord Curzon decided to present one lamp to the Taj Mahal as his gift. His efforts are described by his biographer Lord Ronald Shay:

' "A priest at the altar of Beauty", as he called himself, Lord Curzon decided that he would himself select and present a hanging lamp worthy of the building and in 1905, he sought the assistance of Lord Cromer, the British Ambassador to Egypt. "I want to give a beautiful silver hanging lamp of Saracenic design to be hung above the cenotaphs of Shah Jahan and his Queen in the upper mausoleum of the Taj", he wrote to the envoy, and continued, "I have been trying for years to get the people here to give me a design, but have failed. I turn therefore to Cairo, where my recollection is that very beautiful lamps still hang in the Arab mosques." For six months, he carried on a correspondence with Lord Cromer and other authorities in Egypt and failing to obtain what he wanted by this means, he decided to visit Cairo on his way

A British Viceroy's Tribute to a Mughal Empress 83

home in order to see to the matter himself.'

According to his biographer, Lord Ronald Shay, he did this at the end of the following November, and there now hangs from the central dome of the Taj Mahal, the beautiful lamp which he was at last successful in procuring.

The history of the lamp is interesting. The model Lord Curzon sought was hard to find. As a result of the enquiries he made in Cairo, his decision was finally cast in favour of a lamp which was known to have hung in the mosque of Sultan Beyfars II. The lamp itself had vanished and neither in the museums of Cairo, Paris or London, could the original be found. It had probably passed into some private collection, where it was lost to the view of general public.

Fortunately, its features, down to the minutest details, were well known and having arrived at the decision to have a copy made, Lord Curzon sought the advice of two experts, Herz Bey — the Director of the Arab Museum at Cairo and E. Richmond of the Egyptian Public Works Department, as to the best means of making the lamp. It then became apparent that there were just two men in Egypt, who were considered capable of carrying out a work of so much delicacy.

Finally, the choice fell upon Todros Badir, who at the end of two years of labour, produced a lamp in bronze, inlaid throughout with silver and gold, a lamp such as had not been seen since the period of the original, many centuries before. It was typical of Lord Curzon's minute attention to detail, that during this time he had the inscription, with which he desired to commemorate this gift, 'Presented to the Tomb of Mumtaz Mahal by Lord Curzon, Viceroy of India in 1906', to be translated into Persian and then converted by a calligrapher in Agra into one of the scripts employed on the tombs of Shah Jahan and his Queen. The calligraphed inscription was then sent to Cairo for such revision as was necessary to bring it into harmony with the style of the lamp, and finally the words were engraved into a belt of pierced metal round its circumference.

It was rather unfortunate that Lord Curzon was unable to be present at the formal presentation of the lamp as the scene, on the occasion of its installation by Sir John Hewett, Lieutenant Governor of United Provinces and a former colleague of Lord Curzon, was one which would have made a powerful appeal to Lord Curzon's ingrained sense of romance.

A crowd estimated in thousands was present in 1909, to witness the ceremony and the President of Anjuman Islamia, a premier Muslim cultural organisation, fervently thanked the Viceroy for his munificent gift. 'The Taj Mahal is for us, the perfection of Muslim architecture and the embodiment of all that was best in the lives and thoughts of the Mughals' he said, 'It is with feelings of intense gratification that we have watched this cherished mausoleum rescued from neglect and decay, that we have seen the tomb, the mosque and many other structures grouped around it all, tenderly and reverently repaired, the gardens once more assuming their ancient charm and the arcaded court and approaches restored to their former glory.'

'As it [the lamp] hangs above the graves of Mumtaz Mahal and Shah Jahan, it revived in spirit, if not in precise detail, a ceremony performed in olden days, that of lighting up the tomb once a year on the anniversary of the Emperor's death. The gift could not therefore appeal more strongly to our sentiment and imagination, for this pious usage of honouring the Imperial Dead had disappeared perforce with the passing of the Mughal power and the spoilation of the building at the hands of the invaders.'

Lord Curzon himself echoed these sentiments in his letter to the Governor, 'In asking you to see to its final installation, I would beg that it may be carefully guarded by the custodians of the shrine and may hang there as my last tribute of respect to the glories of Agra, which float like a vision of eternal beauty in my memory and the grave and potent religion, which is professed by so many millions of our fellow subjects in India.'

Today, the famous lamp estimated to be worth Rs. 10,000 in 1909 and Rs. 2.25 million in 1995, hangs over the cenotaph of the Empress Mumtaz Mahal. Years of exposure to the weather have tarnished the lamp and it is a pity that it is not kept well-polished. But for ages to come, it will hang there as the tribute of a British Viceroy to a Mughal Empress.

Treasures of the Last Peshwa

The last of the Peshwas, the defacto rulers of the Maratha empire in India, Baji Rao II or 'Badgee Rao' as the British liked to refer to him, became a British prisoner after the battle of Seoni in 1818. Among the six conditions the British imposed on the erstwhile potentate, was that he must relinquish the title of Peshwa, retire with all his treasures to a place far away from his domains 'without a day's delay' and that in return an annual pension of eight lakhs rupees (800,000) would be paid to him till his death. Having granted the pension, the British then felt that they had been too generous to the Peshwa, although British historians acknowledge that for an ex-ruler of the importance of the Peshwa, whose territories fetched an annual income of Rs. 97,00,000 in those halcyon days, eight lakhs rupees less than one tenth the territorial revenue, was not in fact very much.

The ex-Peshwa was finally asked by the British to settle down in Bithoor, near modern Kanpur, and the exiled prince lived in this town for thirty-three years, surrounded by a retinue of 15,000 adherents. But when he died in 1851, the vast treasures of the Peshwa had vanished: even the British, who had spies in the Peshwa's innermost councils, were unable to discover what had happened to the wealth. Now, in free India, a century and half later, thanks to the efforts of many eminent scholars, we are able to discover the ultimate fate of the fabulous treasures of the Maratha empire.

As the doyen among Maratha princes, Baji Rao II, even during his exile, spent lavishly on charities (on an average Rs. 400,000 annually). According to economists, a real silver rupee of those days had eighty times the purchasing power of today and for ten silver rupees, one could buy a gold sovereign. One reason for the Peshwa's extravagance was that he was convinced that the pension of Rs. 800,000 given to him, would be made available to his successors also and therefore there was no imperative need to leave behind anything out of this stipend. Thus, when he died in 1851, the treasury was empty; in fact the accounts revealed a debt of Rs. 400,000.

The treasures in his palace (built as a copy of the famous Shanwarwada palace in Poona) comprised Rs. 16,00,000 worth of valuable English East India Company bonds, fetching a return of 5 per cent; gem-studded jewels valued at Rs. 1,000,000; gold ornaments at Rs. 60,000; Rs. 300,000 worth of gold bullion, silver plate and ornaments worth Rs. 20,000. But no one believed that the Peshwa's treasures

Nana Saheb Peshwa

could be so paltry. Of the Rs. 300,000 worth of gold mohurs, the funeral ceremonies of the ex-Peshwa incurred an expenditure of two-thirds of this amount and when the potentate's adopted son, the famous Nana Saheb, took over the management of the properties, he found that his income was likely to be half his estimated expenses, especially as the British informed him that the annual pension of Rs. 800,000 would no longer be granted.

Nevertheless, Nana Saheb appealed to the British for the continuance of the stipend. However, the Governor General decided that such a pension would be 'uncalled for and unreasonable', since the last Peshwa had received the amount of Rs. 800,000 per annum for thirty-three years, besides the proceeds of his ancestral jaghir (estate). Thus, over a period of nearly one-third of a century, almost two and half crores of rupees had been spent on the exiled prince, who in the words of the Governor General, 'had no charges to maintain, no sons of his own and had left property worth Rs. 28 lakhs for his family ...' Further, the British were of the opinion that, 'in all probability, the property left is really much larger than it is avowed to be.'

Deprived of his pension, Nana Saheb found that even his claim to the property left by his adopted father was being disputed by interested parties, among them a lady, known as Maharani Yasoda Bai, who claimed to be the wife of an earlier Peshwa. Further, as the years went by, the British even denied to him the title of Maharaja and in 1857, the bitter scion of the Peshwas, decided to play a prominent part in the First War of Indian Independence, known to the British as the Sepoy Mutiny. The failure of this war, made it necessary for the Indian prince to abandon his palace. As British troops neared Bithoor, Nana Saheb divided his wealth into three portions. Heavy treasures like gold coins and silver howdahs (sofas used on elephant back), he decided to dump into the wells of the palace at Bithoor. The sacred treasures of the Peshwa family, such as the vestments of Saint Ramdas, the preceptor of the great Shivaji, founder of the Maratha empire, were to be submerged in the waters of the nearby sacred river, so that they would not fall into unworthy hands. As to the fabulous jewellery of the Marathas, Nana Saheb decided to take these treasures with him and the British writer, Percival Landon, notes that eight elephants carried the treasures of the Indian leader as he crossed into Nepal.

Entering Bithoor, the British troops systematically looted Nana Saheb's palace. Many British soldiers believed that the thick walls of the Bithoor Palace contained numerous hiding places for the treasures and so destroyed the edifice brick by brick. Ironically, such destruction made it impossible for the official Prize Agents of the British Army to identify later, the treasury sections of the palace, where such wealth might have been hidden.

But a traitrous Indian spy, Angoori Tiwary, brought to the knowledge of the British, that one of the seven deep wells within the palace contained abandoned bullion. Using hundreds of British soldiers, Lt. Malcolm of the Royal Engineers, drained the well and took out what is called 'Nana's gold plate'. According to a contemporary British historian, 'this was immensely valuable because it was of solid and very pure gold, but it had no artistic importance'. After ten days of salvage work, the British withdrew the silver howdah of Baji Rao and great quantities of silver plate, totalling in all Rs. 10 million.

Below the silverware was found bullion in an immense number of ammunition boxes, closely packed with gold mohur and silver coins, totalling Rs. 3,000,000. The well had yielded wealth valued at Rs. 13 million equivalent to Rs. 1040 million in 1995. The British soldiers had worked under strenuous conditions to retrieve the so-called 'rebel's wealth', hoping that it would be declared prize money. This would have meant at least Rs. 1000 per soldier. But the Governor General decreed that the immense treasure did not fall under the category of captured enemy prize. The soldiers got nothing.

Nana Saheb fled to Nepal and sought asylum with the Nepalese rulers. He found that the Prime Minister of Nepal, Jung Bahadur, attempting to take advantage of the situation, offered ridiculously low prices for the Maratha jewels. For example, the fabulous *Naulakha har*, a necklace comprising of pearls, emeralds and diamonds of immense size, had to be sold to the Nepalese Prime Minister for a paltry Rs. 93,000, less than one tenth of its value. Later, Jung Bahadur took pity on the exiled leader's family and in lieu of monetary payment for the jewels, gave eight villages, with an annual income of Rs. 8,000, to the principal wife of Nana Saheb. These jaghirs remained with the lady till her death in 1896, when the Nepalese Durbar took over the property.

Still the stories about the vast wealth of the Peshwas, concealed in unknown corners of rural Kanpur, persisted and in later years the British Government permitted one of the wives of a former Peshwa, Maharani Yasoda Bai, to take the help of the British Army to recover certain treasures of the Peshwas, hidden in underground chambers near Kanpur. The only condition imposed for such aid, was that the British Government was to be given half the treasures found. But the lady soon found that her British friends were attempting to recover the treasures on their own, and therefore, abandoned all efforts, lest the *feringhee* should take away all the 'Peshwa's Treasures'.

The Sepoy Mutiny of 1857 as seen by Queen Victoria

Ever since the reign of George III in the 18th century, every day a special courier carries a number of red leather boxes from the British Prime Minister's residence to the palace of the British Sovereign. These red leather boxes, sealed with the emblem of the Sovereign, are known as Royal Despatch Bags and contain documents with the advice of the British Prime Minister relating to matters that affect the 'British Empire' and perusing them constitutes the most important task of the monarch of Great Britain. These despatches are considered to be so confidential, that even the Prince of Wales, is not allowed to open the boxes. Reading one of the despatches on June 8, 1857, Queen Victoria found a memorandum from the Prime Minister Lord Palmerston, that 'widespread mutiny and dissatisfaction among the native troops of India is reported and it is hoped that the situation will be controlled'.

This was the very first indication Queen Victoria received of the Sepoy Mutiny (known to Indian nationalists as the First

War of Independence), although as early as December 1856, her husband, Prince Albert had predicted the possibilities of such an emergency, and had warned the British Cabinet that the Indian subcontinent was seething with unrest and that the number of British regiments in India should be increased. But Lord Palmerston felt that the Prince's fears were baseless and the ratio of British soldiers to Indian sepoys remained at the usual proportion of one to six.

The Leader of the British opposition, Benjamin Disraeli, had represented to the Queen more than once, that the policy of Doctrine of Lapse pursued by Lord Dalhousie, the Governor General of India in 1855, was sure to bring trouble. The deposition of Wajid Ali Shah, the Nawab of Oudh, was felt by Disraeli to be a particularly wrong step and he pleaded with the Queen that this action would alienate Indian royalty, who now found that their thrones were not safe from the grasp of the East India Company.

The Queen, too, shared Disraeli's apprehensions and had decided that when Lord Dalhousie's tenure ended, the new Governor General should be a person less likely to alienate the Indian rulers. But since the Constitution of the East India Company gave administrative rights of the Indian Empire to the Board of Directors of the East India Company, the Queen was unable to enforce her decision. It was the right of the Directors to suggest the name of the Governor General-designate and the Queen was merely required to approve it.

The Board of Directors chose Lord Canning, a comparatively unknown man and sent his name to the Queen for approval. The Queen was very much annoyed at this and wrote to the Directors, that while she concurred with their decision to avoid causing embarrassment to Lord Canning, in future, she would not agree to a selection in which she had no say. But as events proved themselves, the Queen herself could not have made a better choice than the Board did.

The Sepoy Mutiny of 1857 as seen by Queen Victoria

Meanwhile, India throbbed with freedom fever and in the dusty glare of 1857, odd tales ran through the villages, as runners flitted by and the tale of greased cartridges spread and continued to keep spreading. The news that cartridges smeared with the fat of pigs and cows were being used to alienate the Indian sepoys from their religious taboos, gathered momentum. In order to load their rifles, the sepoys were required to bite open the fat-smeared cartridges, thus 'polluting' the Hindu, to whom the cow was sacred, and the Muslim, to whom the pig was anathema. But the true import of the conflict had not yet dawned on the British and London was at its gayest. Even the Royal court was extraordinarily brilliant, with the German Crown Prince recently arrived from Berlin to marry the Princess Royal. On June 23, a grand banquet was held in London to celebrate the British victory at Plassey, a hundred years earlier.

Lord Palmerston, the Prime Minister himself, had not been unduly worried by the reports of insurrection and took the first opportunity to assure the Queen that the revolt would be quelled in a few weeks. It was therefore a surprise to the Queen, when the next intelligence from India brought news of the capture of Delhi by the sepoys. The Queen was unaware that the Mughal Emperor of Delhi was to be the titular leader of the revolt and when she heard the Mughal capital had fallen, she felt great

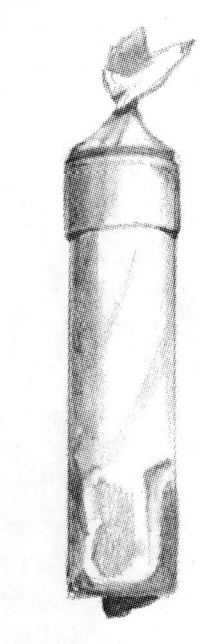

Cartridge that caused the Sepoy Mutiny

anxiety about the welfare of the Mughal royal family.

In common with the average Briton, the Queen suffered acute mental torture, as news of rebel successes continued to arrive. 'We are all in sad anxiety about India, which engrosses all our attention', she wrote to her uncle, King Leopold of Belgium. 'Troops cannot be raised fast or large enough and the horrors committed by the rebels on women and children are unknown in these ages. The reputation of England's power has had rude shock. We have nearly gone to the full extent of our available means and may with difficulty retrieve the situation.' The Sepoy Mutiny was to cost the East India Company 37 million, before it was quelled.

Queen Victoria in 1857

The Sepoy Mutiny of 1857 as seen by Queen Victoria

Besides, the Queen feared that France might attack England at this critical juncture, when all available troops were being sent to India. A few months earlier, the French secret police had traced Orsini, the French anarchist, to British shores and later when it was found that Orsini was the brains behind the attempt to assassinate the French Emperor, feelings ran high against the British. In a formal note the French Government had asked the British Government to discountenance asylum to such anarchists and there was every possibility that the Orsini incident might trigger an Anglo-French war.

Despite this, Queen Victoria maintained cordial relations with Napoleon III, the Emperor of France, and when he heard that the city of Delhi had fallen to the sepoys, the Emperor informed the Queen that he was willing to allow any number of British troops to pass through France, en route to India. But the Queen 'graciously' refused the offer. At the same time, conveying troops to India in ships via the Cape of Good Hope, involved considerable delay and after hearing about the fall of Delhi, the Queen asked her Ambassador in Istanbul, Lord Stratford de Radclyffe, to request the Sultan of Turkey for permission to allow British troops to cross the Isthmus of Suez (the Suez Canal had not been dug in those days). After crossing the Isthmus, steamers were to take the soldiers to India. The Isthmus belonged to Turkey in 1857 and this short cut would have enabled the soldiers to reach India much quicker than by the usual route.

The Sultan agreed to the request and ordered his Viceroy, the Khedive of Egypt, to extend the British all facilities to march across the area. From then on, till the end of the Mutiny, Suez Isthmus became the transhipment point for news and Army personnel. In her anxiety to obtain news from India, the Queen found it difficult to wait till the official intelligence arrived twice a month by sea mail. She directed that the ships carrying official news from India must touch

Trieste in Italy and the British Consul at Trieste was to send a resume of the news by the recently invented telegraph. Couriers arriving with information about the Mutiny were to be send immediately to the Palace. The Queen, with the Prince Consort, spent hours before a map of India, marking the fortunes of the British Army with paper flags. Officers arriving from India were asked to come to the Palace to give their personal accounts of the holocaust.

General Campbell, coming to see the Queen prior to his departure for India, found her so anxious about the insurrection, that he assured her that he would be proceeding directly from the Palace to the ship that was to take him to India. Hundreds of petitions reached the Queen from the relations of soldiers stationed in India, requesting her to force the British Cabinet to take more speedy measures to send succour to British soldiers, India being the place where everyone had been anxious to place a son. These letters intensified the Queen's acute mental anguish and she pestered the Cabinet ministers to take immediate steps to suppress the rebellion with all available speed. The Prime Minister resented this nagging and wrote her a sarcastic letter in which he averred that he was fortunate that the Queen was not the Leader of the Opposition in the British Parliament.

At the same time, he reminded her that there was nothing to be gained by rushing more troops to India and that 'measures were sometimes best calculated to succeed, which follow others step by step'. The British public, however, were unaware of her anxieties and underestimated her vigilance, for when, towards the end of August, she left her palace at Osborne to go to her mansion at Balmoral for her autumn holidays, protests were raised against her action. 'Parliament is still sitting', the newspapers argued, 'and the Queen's withdrawal to the North before its prorogation in the midst of the Indian peril is regrettable. The affairs of the nation must on no account yield to the convenience of her private affairs.'

But there was little justification for this reproach and throughout her sojourn at Balmoral, little else except India occupied her mind. She vividly felt the added anxieties due to the distance from the seat of danger and the difficulty of communication. Prince Albert, in one of his letters to Lord Stockmar, from Balmoral, remarked that the spectre of the Indian Mutiny was always before them in England.

The royal families of Europe were not slow in offering forces for service in India and King Leopold of Belgium, wrote to the Queen that his Government was willing to send some troops to India to quell the Mutiny. On receiving the letter, Queen Victoria summoned Lord Palmerston and sought his opinion. Palmerston felt that it would be disastrous for England, if Indian troops discovered that Britain was obliged to accept the help of other nations to withstand their assault. He therefore advised the Queen to politely reject the offer.

As the tension and feeling against the rebels in India mounted among the British, the handful of Indians in Britain, mostly Indian Princes, deprived of their territory by the East India Company and exiled by the British Government from India, found themselves the target of British fanatics. The worst to suffer was Maharaja Duleep Singh, the son of Maharaja Ranjit Singh (1779-1839), the famous Lion of Punjab and the last independent ruler of the Sikh state. Maharaja Duleep Singh had been taken to England by the British after the defeat of the Punjab Sikh Army in the British-Sikh Wars of 1845, and now, even the members of the British House of Commons found it difficult to control their animosity against him.

But they knew that the Maharaja was a special protégé of the Queen and that she would disapprove of any hostility directed against him. Lord Clarendon, a British Peer tried to antagonise the Queen against the Maharaja by writing to her: 'I am sorry to learn that the Maharaja had shown little or no regrets for the atrocities, which have been committed by the Indians and from what I hear, he is either from nature or by early education very cruel'. The Queen, it must be noted in her favour, did not share this view. 'I am very much surprised at your observation', she wrote back to Lord Clarendon. 'It is hardly to be expected that he, a deposed Indian Sovereign not very fond of British Rule as represented by the East India Company should like his countrymen called fiends and monsters and to see them brought in thousands to be executed. His best course is to say nothing.'

By September 1857, it became apparent to the British Cabinet that the situation in India might have got out of control and that it would be judicious to prepare the British nation for the worst consequences. The Prime Minister decided that a day must be set apart as National Prayer Day, so that the people would realise that their sovereignity over India was in jeopardy and wrote to the Queen for permission to proclaim September 11, 1857, as the Day. But the Queen felt that while it was appropriate that a day be set apart for national mourning, the name ought to be more befitting and suggested that October 11, 1857, must be designated the 'Day of Prayer and Intercession'.

But as the months rolled by, due largely to the lethargy displayed by the majority of Indian Princes, the Sepoy Mutiny began to peter out and the fall of Delhi to British forces on September 14, 1857, marked the beginning of the end of the revolt. The first to congratulate the Queen was the Emperor of France, who sent her a telegram after hearing about the capture of Delhi by British forces.

As the embers of the Mutiny began to die down, all the problems which had been so far relegated to the background came to the fore. The first of these to come to the attention of the Queen, was the future of the East India Company. The Company had been founded under Queen Elizabeth I in 1600 AD, remodelled under Queen Anne in the 18th century and it now awaited dismemberment under Queen Victoria. That the vast Empire, which had grown up in the East should be governed by the British Government, through a body which was nominally a commercial corporation, had long been an anachronism and the Indian Mutiny gave the death blow to the system.

Now that the Empire was directly under her Rule, the Queen decided to issue a formal Proclamation to the Indian Nation to convey her warm feeling towards it. Accordingly, she requested Lord Derby to compose a Proclamation, '... in his excellent English, bearing in mind that it is a female Sovereign, who speaks to more than hundred millions of Eastern People, after a bloody Civil War. Such a document should breathe feelings of generosity, benevolence and religious feeling'. As far as she was concerned, the Indian Sepoy Mutiny was over.

The Martyr-Emperor's Unfulfilled Wish

A few years after Napoleon's demise, the French prevailed on their former enemies, the British, to hand over the great hero's remains for enshrinement in the French National Valhalla. In 1965, half a century after the execution of the Irish patriot Roger Casement, in Britain, the Irish compelled the British to return to them the body for burial in Irish soil.

But more than 130 years after his death in exile and despite five decades of Indian freedom, the body of the last Mughal Emperor, Bahadur Shah Zafar, the titular leader of the First War of Indian Independence (Sepoy Mutiny), still lies in an obscure grave in Rangoon, Burma, and his prophetic couplet, 'The broken remnants of Zafar's grave have been stamped out into total oblivion. Where shall his well-wishers go to say prayers for the peace of his soul?', is a pungent comment on Indian nationalists, all the more so, as Bahadur Shah himself had chosen and reserved a place near Delhi for his burial.

When on May 11, 1857, the sepoys arrived from the Meerut cantonment to proclaim him the Mughal Emperor of India and the focal point of the freedom struggle, Bahadur Shah was dazed by the turn of events. The British had earlier considered that there was no reason to maintain even the title of King of Delhi for the Mughal (far less that of Emperor) and had decided to deny even the right of residence in the Red Fort to Bahadur Shah's descendants. They were to be sent away to the Delhi suburb of Mehrauli and to be titled Princes of Delhi. The credit for getting him to assume the leadership of the freedom struggle, goes to his Queen Zeenat Mahal. The aged king (he was 82 years old), never had any control over the mutinous Army that wanted him as its head and when by the middle of August 1857, it became certain that Delhi was sure to be captured by the British, Bahadur Shah expressed a great desire to come out of the palace and die fighting. But his extreme age made his ambition futile and he sought asylum in his ancestor Humayun's tomb, in Delhi.

Later, he surrendered to the British on the understanding that his life would be spared and the aged monarch was brought to trial on January 27, 1858, in the royal chambers of his own palace. The charges against him were as follows: making war against the British Government; of abetting rebellion; of proclaiming himself the Sovereign of India; causing or being accessory to the death of 49 people of British or European descent.

The trial lasted 40 days and the Court, composed of only Britishers, found him guilty of the main charges and sentenced him to transportation and exile for life. Originally it was proposed to exile him to South Africa, but as the local government refused him entry, it was decided to send him to Rangoon, in Burma. When the royal prisoner's party left Delhi on October 7, 1858, there were 29 members in it, including the deposed monarch, his two Queens (Zeenat Mahal Begum and Taj Mahal Begum), four concubines, Prince Jawan Bakht and his wife, four male and 11 female attendants. Maharishi Devendranath Tagore, father of the poet Rabindranath Tagore (1862-1941), mentions in his memoirs the fact of his having seen the entire mournful party wending their way to Rangoon. When the party reached Allahabad, five weeks later, 14 of the group (including Taj Mahal Begum and two other concubines), realizing that it was not going to be an easy way of life in Rangoon, deserted and came back to Delhi. It is said, that en route to Rangoon, the Viceroy permitted Nawab Wajid Ali Shah, the deposed ruler of Oudh, to meet the Emperor at Matiaburj, near Calcutta and the former vassal tearfully bade farewell to his ex suzerain, performing the customary 27 salams (honours). Five months later, the group reached Rangoon on April 16, 1859, and under heavy military guard, the exiles began their life in a double-storeyed wooden structure near the race course. The only outing permitted was to the female members of the party, when the wife of the officer-in-charge of the prison, Captain Davies, took them for a drive.

The last Mughal Emperor Bahadur Shah in exile

The entire party was granted a total monthly pension of Rs. 600 (food allowance at Rs. 11 per day, one rupee extra for feast on Sundays and two rupees per prisoner on the first of each month for toiletries). The broken hearted monarch spent his days nursed by Zeenat Mahal Begum and according to his letter written to his daughter in India, the British never lost a chance to humiliate him. Once the aged Emperor complained of the leaking roof in his bungalow (which had only four serviceable rooms) he was told by the guards not to expect the Red Fort in Rangoon. Another day some Muslim well-wishers presented the fallen Mughal with some gifts and the monarch, as per Mughal custom, asked the Queen to give them one of her jewels as a return gift. As a result, the British further cut down his allowances the next day, 'as a prisoner with such munificence' should not need large monetary allowances.

Finally, when death came to him on November 7, 1862, only Zeenat Mahal Begum, his son Prince Jawan Bakht and his wife and a little granddaughter were present in the room. The Begum was not allowed to accompany the cortege, and the last Mughal Emperor was buried in the compound of the prison. Four years after the royal prisoner's death, the remaining exiles were ordered to take up residence in another house at a reduced pension of Rs. 500. Tragedy struck again when Prince Jawan Bakht died at Moulmein, in 1884, and the last Mughal's surviving descendants scattered to different towns in Burma. Begum Zeenat Mahal died on July 17, 1886, and was buried beside her husband. By then the compound had been leased to a British official, who embarked on a successful policy of obliterating the graves by using the area as a tennis court and horse stable.

The result was that when, at the beginning of the 20th century, some patriotic Indians sought out the graves, it was with great difficulty that they were able to identify them. A tablet was raised on the spot with the words, 'The exiled King of Delhi — Bahadur Shah died at Rangoon on 7.11.1862 and was buried near this place'. A few months later, the date of the Queen's demise was also recorded on the slab.

Some years later, the Government of Burma allowed local Indians to erect an iron structure to mark the spot. After the fall of Burma to the Japanese in 1942, Netaji Subhas Chandra Bose, the Head of the Provisional Government of Free India, built a 'Martyrs Memorial' at the spot, but even this was destroyed by the British when they re-entered Rangoon in 1945. After Indian independence in 1947, the great grandson of Bahadur Shah, Prince Bedar Bakht, approached the Indian Prime Minister, Jawaharlal Nehru, for financial help and a monthly pension of Rs. 500 was granted to him. Today, a modest tomb covers the area where Bahadur Shah Zafar is said to have been buried.

But the descendants of the Mughals have fallen on evil days and according to one historian the last male scion of the Mughals is working as a canteen boy in Saudi Arabia.

When the Indian Prime Minister, Rajiv Gandhi, visited Rangoon in 1988, he made it a point to visit the tomb of Bahadur Shah to offer prayers. Every Friday, as the rest of Rangoon goes about its daily chores, a small crowd gathers at Bahadur Shah's tomb in the centre of the city to seek the blessings of the last Mughal Emperor of India. In recognition of the great symbolic value of the Emperor's tomb, the Government of India funded the construction of a Bahadur Shah Zafar Hall at the site in 1994.

The tomb is situated in an upmarket area of Rangoon and with real estate prices escalating sharply in recent years, could well become an alluring target for property developers. Already the road leading to the tomb, once called Bahadur Shah Zafar Road, has been renamed Jeevaka Road.

The Government of India is aware of public feelings,

regarding the necessity of bringing back the remains of the royal exile, especially as Bahadur Shah Zafar himself had chosen a place at the Dargah (shrine) of Qutb Sahib, near Delhi, for his grave.

The last Mughal Emperor liked the idyllic surroundings near the Qutb Minar and used to often stay near the Dargah. He had an earlier-built palace near the shrine renovated and renamed Zafar Mahal (after his nom-de-plume Zafar, used for his poems). He had decided that his crypt should be inside the 700-year-old shrine of the Saint Khwaja Qutubdin Bhaktiyar Kaki (known as Qutb Sahib) and his final resting place was to be between that of Emperor Shah Alam II (1759-1809) and Emperor Akbar II (1806-1837). But this yawning space between the two graves remains unutilised to date and is a blot on India's national honour. Indeed, as the martyr Emperor himself had prophetically foretold:

'Kitna badnaseeb hai Zafar dafn ke liye,
Do gaz zamin bhi ne mili kue uar mein'

[What an unlucky man Zafar is, He could not get two yards of land to be buried in his beloved country].

October 2, 1869: The Day Mahatma Gandhi was born

It is interesting to consider what the situation in the world was on October 2, 1869, the day Mahatma Gandhi was born. Scarely a dozen years had passed since the First War of Indian Independence (Sepoy Mutiny). The world had just celebrated the first birth centenary of Napoleon Bonaparte, who was born in 1769 and had died fifty-two years later, in 1821. The Suez Canal was in the final stages of construction and its opening in November was eagerly awaited.

A study of the newspapers dealing with October 2, 1869, shows that there was a general atmosphere of peace, as the British Empire was in its heyday. The newspapers were full of details of the disaster to the ship *Carnatic*, which had run aground on the Suez-Bombay run, with a loss of forty lives. It was felt that only an Enquiry Committee would bring to light the causes of the disaster.

The public were informed by the journals, that Dr. Livingstone, the famous missionary-explorer, who had not been heard of for some time from the African wilds, was safe and according to Sir Roderick Murchison, would be reaching West Africa shortly, after crossing the continent. As for the prices of commodities, the best quality Manila cheroots were being sold at Rs. 90 per thousand and the best tobacco at Rs 2 per lb. The Chowk Hotel at Matheran, Bombay, was advertising its rate at Rs 6 per day. Houses were available at Malabar Hill, Bombay, full-sized bungalows, at a rent of Rs 125 to Rs 300 per month. Haircuts seem to have been costly in posh establishments at one and half rupees. Today, when prohibition, one of Mahatma Gandhi's cherished desires, has been thrown overboard, it is pertinent to consider that one dozen bottles of the best Champagne cost Rs 74, and one dozen bottles of sherry Rs 37, in 1869.

British newspapers were eager to have the Kashmir Valley converted into a colony for the British, as the climate there suited them. It was also felt that a general sanitorium should be built there for British personnel and that extensive tracts in the Valley should be bought for British settlers.

Another editor was worried over the likely success or failure of the new Suez Canal. Analysing the economics of the Suez project, he informed the public that out of the 75 million cubic feet of earth to be excavated, only five million remained for removal. The opening date of the Canal was to be November 17, 1969, and it was felt that unless 16 ships of at least 1000 tons each, used the Canal every day, it would be a financial failure.

Regarding more scandalous matters, controversy raged in the pages of a Bombay daily as to whether it was possible for a Goanese butler to acquire Rs. 8,000 in 13 years, without swindling his master. One scribe, describing himself as the 'True Lover of his Country', felt that such queries damaged the fair name of Goans. *The Times of India*, Bombay, dated October 2, carried an advertisement by one Dossa Hariram, who warned people against dealing with his sons, saying that he would not be responsible for the transactions.

The upcountry journals regularly published excerpts from the *True Story of Lady Byron*, as revealed by her diaries and social circles exulted in the whiff of scandal it contained.

Just like the Stock Market scams which plagued India a century and a quarter later, Bombay was agog with the Premchand Roychand affair. What transpired was that the famous business house of Premchand Roychand, dealing in cotton, was about to declare insolvency when the Bank of Bombay, the leading financial institution of the city, discovered that were the eminent Indian business house to fail, it would ruin the market. The Bank, therefore, advanced Rs. 25,00,000 to the concern, against collateral consisting of property and jewels. But certain citizens smelt a rat in these dealings and the whole affair of the loan was being investigated by a Commission.

One political commentator was happy that famines were occurring in India less frequently. Another British editor was upset at the truculent manner in which the Sheikhs of the Middle East were treating the Indian Government and urged the Indian Navy to take punitive action against them, so that the Viceroy would be more respected in the Persian Gulf area.

In short, this was the state of affairs as reported by the newspapers in India and abroad on October 2, 1869, when in the town of Porbunder in western India, a son was born to Shri Kaba Gandhi and his wife. Little did the proud parents realise that for centuries to come, the boy's birthday would be observed the world over in honour of one of greatest the emanicipators of humanity.

Indian Maharajas: 'After Ambassadors, Before Dukes'

They belong to the vanishing breed of royalty. There were about 565 Princely States and the Indian maharajas ranged from the Nizam of Hyderabad, with territories larger than Great Britain, to small chieftains in Gujarat, with just a few acres as their fiefdoms. But as per records kept by the British Government, their ranks and privileges under the category 'India's Native Rulers', were meticulously chronicled forming a veritable Asian *Almanac de Gotha* ... So much so that, when questions were raised as to their place in the protocol for the Coronation celebrations held at the Imperial Capital of London in 1901, their suzerain, Edward VII, King of Great Britain and Emperor of India, unhesitatingly decided that the Indian Maharajas' place in the ceremonies would be, 'After Ambassadors, before Dukes'.

If the Emperor of India was wary of anything about the maharajas, it was only of their fabulous wealth. The venerable Indian newspaper, The *Statesmen* of Calcutta, made a rough

Maharaja Sajjan Singh of Mewar.
A traditional maharaja swathed in diamonds

estimate of their total worth in 1947 as equivalent to US $ 6,000 million, an amount equal to at least US $ 180,000 million in 1996. The eminent Indian historian and author, Manohar Malgonkar, referring to the book, *Cartier — Jeweller Extraordinary*, states that an entire page in the book is devoted to the Maharaja of Baroda, Sir Sayajirao Gaekwar (1862-1939), who scared his suzerains, the British, by planning to make a crown for himself more precious than the Imperial Crown of Emperor George V.

In 1933, Sayajirao commissioned Cartier to design for him a special crown that he could wear for a Durbar (Royal Public Audience) on the occasion of the Diamond Jubilee of his ascending the Baroda throne in 1935. Cartier had been asked to set either one or both of the famous Baroda diamonds in the crown. One was the Star of the South, weighing 125 carats, and the other, the Eugene, was slightly smaller. 'The project was mysteriously dropped', the book states.

Malgonkar states, 'Well... I could have resolved the mystery, for I had read the whole file about the case of the "Arched" crown in the archives of the India Office Library in London, decades later. The Raj's functionaries had gone into a tizzy over what they perceived to be a blatant usurpation of monarchical symbols by an Indian Maharaja. The British Resident at Baroda wrote a frantic letter to the Viceroy that the new crown that Cartier was commissioned to design would not only rival the British Crown in splendour, but, far more unforgiveably, closely resemble it.

'To the guardians of the Raj, the symbols of British royalty were sacrosanct. The Viceroy, in turn, referred the matter to his superior in London, the Secretary of State for India, asking for a ruling. As it turned out, the Secretary too, professed to be shocked at a Maharaja's attempt to arrogate to himself so distinctive a symbol of British royalty, but thought it prudent not to make an issue of it. He actually advised that they should all wait till Maharaja Sayajirao (a very shrewd maverick) died and then tell his heir that he could not wear an Arched crown. While all this went on, broad hints were dropped to make it clear to Sayajirao that his order for a new crown would be looked upon with disfavour by his British suzerain. The "wise" Maharaja took the hint and cancelled the order for the crown.'

Even after Indian independence, the Nizam of Hyderabad, whose wealth in 1945 was estimated at Rs. 9,000 million, continued to head the list. But after the Indian Government peeled off palaces and treasures from his possessions, the Nizam's listed wealth in 1967, was estimated at Rs. 1,500 million (US $ 200 million), besides Trust funds valued at Rs. 375 million (US $ 50 million), his palaces at Hyderabad with curios worth Rs. 60 million (US $ 8 million), and 23,497 acres of cultivable land. The Nizam's jewel collections were then estimated to be worth Rs. 600 million (US $ 80 million) in 1967. Most of the jewels are said to be contained in a safe deposit vault of a Bombay bank while the uncut stones and pearls are thought to be kept in Hyderabad. Of the diamonds, the two most precious stones are the Jacob diamond weighing 187.75 carats and the Nizam diamond weighing 277 carats.

As to who the next richest maharaja was is a debatable question. The ex-rulers of Jaipur, Gwalior and Baroda, were considered to be the prime contenders. In the case of Baroda, we have more reliable information as he was known as the eighth richest man in the world in the 1930s, said to be worth Rs. 2,250 million (nearly US $ 700 million in those halcyon days). The State jewels of the Maharaja at the Nazar Bagh Palace in Baroda, were worth more than Rs. 30 million and one seven-strand pearl necklace alone was worth Rs. 4.5 million (US $ 1.35 million), the central diamond being valued at over Rs. 1.12 million (US $ 336,000). This diamond was the famous Star of the South, found in Brazil in 1883. The fabulous wealth of the Baroda royal family had been carefully conserved by Sir Sayajirao, who was so frugal that he once told a courtier that while he was willing to sign a cheque on the spot for Rs. 6 million (US $ 1.8 million) for a worthy cause, he was not willing to spend a rupee (30 cents) uselessly. But his grandson, Sir Pratap Singh who succeeded him, had no such scruples and in 1948, in an effort to rival the Aga Khan, spent Rs. 6 million to acquire the famous Kidare stud in UK, besides purchasing 53 thoroughbred horses. At the same time, he had 80 horses in his own stables in India, under the care of 150 stablehands.

Prior to 1971, 114 of the Indian maharajas were entitled to be addressed as His Highness, in addition to titular designations like Nizam, Nawab, Maharaja, Maharana, Jamsahib and so on. Today, five decades after Indian independence, they still make news. But officially, there are no Maharajas in India.

What has happened to their wealth, often accumulated over centuries ...? In 1947-48, the Government of India separated the personal wealth of the Indian Princes from State Regalia such as the crown throne/sceptres (which cannot be sold off) and the official list is with the Home Ministry.

While the British, during their rule, allowed the Indian Princely families to maintain their domains and wealth separately, independent India incorporated their kingdoms into the country in 1947. In return, they were allowed to keep their titles, some of their palaces, many of their jewels and were granted annual allowances called Privy Purses, which in total amounted to about Rs. 200 million (US $ 60 million). In 1948, this amount was divided among 550 of them, ranging from Rs. 20 million (US $ 1.5 million) for the Nizam of Hyderabad to less than US $ 10 for some of the junior-most chieftains of Gujarat.

Princes with 19 gun salutes or more did not have to pay any customs duty on goods imported by them for their personal use or for the use of any members of their families. They were entitled to operate their foreign exchange holdings (which they held prior to the merger of their States with India) without any reference to Government of India regulations. In 1962, foreign exchange held privately by the Indian princes was estimated at Rs. 1,050 million (US $ 140 million and the equivalent of US $ 560 million in 1995). By 1961, the princes had so carefully camouflaged their wealth that only 16 of them figured in the Finance Ministry's official list as persons with an income exceeding Rs. 11 million (US $ 1.5 million) annually. By 1968, the list had dwindled to eight. In order to build up a 'Maharaja lobby', between 1947 and 1971 some of them entered the Indian Parliament as elected members. Maharani Gayatri Devi of Jaipur (acclaimed by Cecil Beaton, the international photographer, as one of the five most beautiful women in 1940) was the most well-known among Indian royalty elected to parliament before 1971.

But in 1971, Prime Minister Indira Gandhi, as a populist measure, persuaded the Indian Parliament to enact a constitutional amendment stripping the Maharajas, Maharanis, Nizams, and Nawabs of their titles, Privy Purses and many of their land holdings. To understand why the high have fallen so low, one must examine the uneasy relationship between one of the most poverty stricken nations in the world and its princely past. While the British allowed the Indian princely families to maintain their domains and wealth during their rule, India in 1971 made them into plain citizens.

As plain 'Mr Indian', the maharajas have now to cope with tax problems, like any other Indian citizen. This in turn has triggered many court battles between the various scions of erstwhile royal families. In the court case involving the Jaipur royal family (as in the case of dozens of other royal families), the issue is a legal debate over whether the eldest son of a former maharaja should inherit his father's property under the millenniums-old law of primogeniture, which would have made him a maharaja in pre-1947, or whether he should get only a share along with his other siblings and his mother/step mothers, as per modern Indian law.

In their former fiefdoms, their erstwhile subjects still regard the former maharajas with great respect. But decades of democracy seem to have gradually dimmed their ancient glory and in 1989 and 1991, many of the former rulers who stood for elections to the Indian parliament, tasted defeat. For the first time, famous names like Jaipur, Mysore and Pataudi, were of no avail against the upsurge of socially aware voters.

Many of the ex-rulers have followed European royalty in converting their palaces into hotels. As some of the palaces, like the Laxmi Vilas Palace of Baroda, had frontages twice that of Buckingham Palace, their maintenance has become a problem for the present impoverished maharajas. Recently, the ex-Maharaja of Mysore decided to convert his exquisite Bangalore Palace, modelled on Britain's Windsor Castle, into a heritage hotel.

According to a news item in the Indian media, the famous palaces of the Nizam of Hyderabad will soon be converted into heritage hotels. Of these, the Faluknuma, situated 2,000 feet above sea level, was built of Italian marble in 1883 and boasts of the world's longest dining table capable of seating 103 diners. In his heyday, the sixth Nizam, Mahbub Ali Khan, would sit at the centre of the table, in a chair distinguished by its arm rests which are at least two inches higher than the rest of the chairs.

The other famous palace of the Nizams, the Chowmohalla, is perhaps the most historically important one. Built between 1724-48, and designed according to Persian architecture, every brick and stone has a tale to tell of the legendary Nizams.

The more ancient Purani Haveli's cachet stems from the fact that the seventh Nizam, Mir Osman Ali Khan, who was in his day the richest man in the world, resided there. It was here too, that his father, the flamboyant sixth Nizam, Mir Mahbub Ali Khan, built the world's largest wardrobe — 240 feet long. But the most beautiful among the grand mansions converted into hotels is the four-century-old Lake Palace, owned by the former Maharana of Udaipur.

The present 'Maharana' is, incidentally, 76th in the line

of Udaipur rulers, with a lineage dating back to 568 AD. This would seem ancient enough. But there are one or two other erstwhile royal clans, such as the princely family of Tripura in north east India, who claim even more hoary ancestry. As an interesting aside, one of the princes from lesser known royalty, the Rajas of Kalakankar in central India became a communist, went to Moscow and eventually married Svetlana, the daughter of the Russian dictator Stalin. The prince died and it was during her visit to India after his death, to visit his family, that Svetlana defected to USA.

Till the 1970s a number of these princes served as India's Ambassadors to various countries. The Maharaja of Jaipur was the envoy to Spain, the Maharaja of Patiala to Italy and the Raja of Aundh served as the Indian High Commissioner to Kenya and Great Britain... They were very much at ease in these international capitals, as there were no Dukes, Earls, Marquis or Counts who could outrank them, either as diplomats or as individuals. During the grant official meets, all eyes turned towards them, as the hosts addressed them as 'Your Highness'.

Many of the present heirs of these once multi-millionaire Indian royal families, have wisely invested in business and helped by the Indian Heritage Commission efforts are being made to preserve the centuries-old palaces, many with walls of filigreed marble and gold painted audience halls. Very few of them are able to spend '800 dollars per day for their underwear', as the Maharaja of Patiala used to do in the 1920s.

Most of these former rulers have been very considerate to their erstwhile servants, who often numbered in the thousands — ranging from grass cutters in the palace lawns (the Maharaja of Jaipur had 400 of them for each of his grand palaces) to Keepers of the Royal Mace. They have created trusts for the workers' retirement, re-educated the retainers to follow new careers so that the snuffing out of royal patronage would not result in utter poverty for the servants ... a case of *noblesse oblige* ...

But it has been difficult to keep up the *noblesse oblige* spirit of past eras due to the loss of their States and Privy Purses. In the last 40 years, a considerable number of hoary heirlooms have been spirited abroad and sold in the auction houses of USA, Britain and Germany. This was done legally in many cases, as the Indian Government, faced with these treasures being melted down for their gold/silver/precious stones, passed a law that 'personal treasures' could be sold if the sale price in hard currency was brought back to India. Only in recent years has the Government of India invoked a law preventing any antique more than hundred years old from being sold outside India.

The sale of these fabulous jewels often produced awkward situations for their buyers. Three decades ago, during a grand ball in Paris, as the Duchess of Windsor made a grand entry wearing a dazzling necklace of diamonds, one of the guests turned to her neighbour, the former Maharani of Baroda and exclaimed, 'Is not the necklace marvellous?' 'Yes ... I know', the ex-Maharani replied frigidly, 'those diamonds were part of my anklet once!' Gossip mongers carried this satirical comment to the Duchess, who was furious at the slight and returned the necklace to the jeweller, the famous Harry Winston of New York, with the warning that she did not want any 'remnants' in her jewellery collection.

Again in 1990, the Government of India intervened in the sale of a gold coin, by a famous auction house in Geneva. This coin, minted in the 17th century by the Mughal Emperor as a birthday souvenir, weighed 10 kg, the heaviest known coin in the world. It was being sold by the 59-year-old ex-Nizam of Hyderabad, hard up to maintain his hundred-thousand-acres sheep ranch in Australia. When last heard of,

Maharaja Ranjit Singh of Nawanagar

the coin was still in Swiss Court custody as it was not clear whether it had been taken out of India before Indian independence in 1947 or later, as the Indian export restrictions on antiques are applicable only on treasures taken out after August 15, 1947. The Nizam claimed that his mother, Princess Niloufer (the daughter of the last Sultan of Turkey), had taken it out of India before the crucial date.

The diamond and gold buckle of a belt which weighs 978.75 (with diamonds evaluated at 638 carats), was acquired by the Government of India for US $ 1.5 million for the National Museum at New Delhi in late 1994, after a national uproar in the media when it became known that it was being offered to Arab millionaires. The international market value of the buckle is US $ 9 million.

Similarly, many historic items like the nine-strand pearl necklace of the Maharajas of Baroda, the fabulous diamond collar (known in the 1920s as the costliest necklace ever made) of the famous cricketer Maharaja Ranjit Singh of Jamnagar and the priceless emeralds of the Rewa royal family, are all treasures that have been lost to India. But whether as Central Government ministers (like the ex-Maharajas of Kashmir and Gwalior) or as commercial magnates, or members of the Indian Parliament or sportsmen, these members of 'royalty of a by-gone era', are very much part of the legendary patina of India's heritage.

Excerpted from the forthcoming book "After Ambassacdors, Before Dukes" by K.R.N. Swamy & Meera Ravi. ISBN 81-85796-05-X.

A British View of the Jallianwala Bagh Massacre

Long before Lidice, Sharpeville and Budapest became synonymous with nationalists braving the armed might of the tyrant, Jallianwala Bagh in Punjab had become a byword for repression. When on April 13, 1919, 379 unarmed civilians were mowed down and 1500 more wounded, under orders of General Dyer of the British Indian Army, even the British *Times* was forced to query: 'How is it that a British General can inflict 2000 casualties on an unarmed mob in the Punjab without the full facts being handed to the Secretary of State for India?' and Indo-British relations changed forever.

Indians are aware of the full implications of the Jallianwala Bagh massacre and the garden has now become a national shrine. But what did the British think of the incident and what actually transpired in British ruling circles, when 'General Dyer shot away more of the British Empire than he preserved'?

India is independent today and the sun has set on the British Empire. Eight decades after the event, many of the

A British View of the Jallianwala Bagh Massacre

British satraps who deified General Dyer are dead but have left accounts of the incident and thanks to eminent authors and journalists like Arthur Swinson, Rupert Furneaux, Ian Colvin and Edward Thompson, with their biographies of British statesmen and Generals of the 1920s, we are able to reconstruct the British view of the tragedy.

British historians no longer believe General Dyer to be a great hero, motivated by a desire to save the British Raj by his ruthless actions. In fact, it is thought that Dyer did not know about the lack of exits from the Jallianwalabagh and as he fired into the crowd, he mistook the action of the crowd in rushing forward to be an attack on himself.

Hence, he directed his bullets 'where the crowd was the thickest'. In this context, years later, the Deputy Commissioner of Amritsar, Miles Irving, was asked by journalist Edward Thompson, what had been the first remark made to him by General Dyer after the firing? Irving replied, 'Dyer came to me all dazed and shaken up and said "I never knew that there

General Dyer

was no way out" '. Quite a different response to the one he gave during the Hunter Enquiry, when he said, 'I had made up my mind that I would do all men to death if they were going to continue the meeting'. General Dyer further told P.G. Puckle, Financial Secretary to the Punjab Government, six months later, 'I have not had a night's sleep since that happened. I keep seeing it all over again.'

General Dyer, despite the adulation the imperialist diehards lavished on him, knew no respite from his conscience. To his daughter-in-law, who comforting him a few days before his death on July 23, 1925, he said, 'Thank you, but I do not want to get better ... So many people who knew the conditions in Amritsar say I did right, but so many others say I did wrong. I only want to die and know from my Maker, whether I did right or wrong.'

General Dyer was suffering so seriously from arterial sclerosis (hardening of the arteries) during his military command of Amritsar, that he was temporarily insane during the firing. The Dyer family itself was under no illusion that the massacre was justified, and in the words of his son Rex Dyer, 'It was a brutal, horrific episode and to pretend otherwise is quite stupid'. *The Encyclopaedia Britannica* opines that Dyer's subsequent bravado was only a mask and he knew that he had committed a great crime.

Sir Michael O'Dwyer, the Lieutenant Governor of Punjab, had backed General Dyer to the hilt and one of the earliest appreciations Dyer received was from him to say, 'Your action correct. Lieutenant Governor approves'. But O'Dwyer later stated that he gave permission for the words 'Lieutenant Governor approves' with reluctance and entirely based on the fact that the military superiors of Dyer had already approved his action.

Later, O'Dwyer had occasion to doubt the sanity of Dyer's action, when the General issued the infamous crawling order by which every Indian entering a certain lane (in which a European missionary lady had been assaulted), had to crawl through on all fours. The Viceroy himself brought the infamous order to the attention of the Lieutenant Governor and O'Dwyer wrote back, 'The order gave me as much of a shock as it did to your Excellency.'

As for the Secretary of State, Mr. Edwin Montague, he later deeply regretted that the Government of India had treated Sir O'Dwyer with kid gloves and felt that the Odwyerism or 'that what the masses call a strong Government is very largely responsible for what has occurred.' After the Hunter Enquiry had completed its report, the Secretary of State wrote to the Viceroy, Lord Chelmsford, saying 'I regret more than anything else, now that I know the sort of man he is, is that we did not deal more severely with O'Dwyer.'

As for the Government of India, under whose very nose (as it was summer and the Indian Government had shifted to the summer capital of Simla in the Punjab), the tragedy occurred, it is shocking to learn from Lord Meston, a member of the Indian Government in those days, that despite the fact he agreed to the imposition of martial law in Amritsar, the Government were unaware of the full details of the tragedy till Dyer sent his report in August, a month later. Lord Meston himself had taken the 200 casualties mentioned by Dyer to mean 50 killed and 150 wounded, as per the 'ordinary ratio'. Lord Meston added that the message of the Lt. Governor approving Dyer, was sent in complete ignorance of the entire circumstances.

Another facet of the Hunter Enquiry that shocked the imperialists, was the 'off handed' manner the Army Headquarters in India treated Dyer after the enquiry. Why did the Army drop General Dyer like a hot potato, after initially hailing him as a 'Savior of India'? The top echelons of the Indian Army, who handled the Dyer case, stated decades later, that the Army Headquarters had earlier decided to back Dyer against any political pressure.

But, when they heard Dyer extolling his action and stating that he had decided to fire even before he reached the Bagh, and that if he had been able to get the armoured cars into the Bagh, he would have used the machine guns and caused even greater slaughter, the top Army brass decided that no one could protect such a foolhardy witness.

Edwin Montague, as the Secretary of State, had the unenviable task of trying to protect the Government of India in the British Parliament and even by November 16, six months after the massacre, Parliament did not have a report on the tragedy. Montague himself had no sympathy for Dyer, about whom he wrote in July 1919 to the Viceroy, '... It was the savage and inappropriate folly of the order which arouses my anger.'

Another participant in the tragic drama was Winston Churchill, who as Defence Minister of Great Britain, had to urge the Army Council to punish General Dyer. He had a hard time with the imperialist diehards in the Army Council and they, at one stage, even made the new Commander-in-Chief of the Indian Army, Lord Rawlinson, state that he would not go to India if justice was not done to Dyer. Finally, Churchill had to threaten that he would not hesitate to dismiss Dyer from the Army if the Army Council procrastinated and the Army Council concluded that Dyer could not be acquitted of an error of judgement. The C-in-C of India had already denied further employment to Dyer and hence it was decided that Dyer be reverted to half pay and be bypassed for promotion.

The Hunter Enquiry Committee Report stirred bitter acrimony in the British Parliament and later it was alleged, that volume number six, the most important book as to the 'acts behind the Amritsar Massacre', had been kept away from the public. Imperialists allege that this volume contained ample proof that Mahatma Gandhi was involved in the 'disturbances in Amritsar' and that in order not to damage his halo, the Secretary of State had hidden the volume. Although this crucial volume made its appearance in the famous Sir O'Dwyer vs Sir Sankaran Nair defamation case of 1924, no copy of it exists today. Perhaps now that eight decades have elapsed since the tragedy and the 50-year limitation on British State Papers are over, some historian might discover the book in the archives of the British Government.

The World's Seventh Largest Diamond

From time immemorial, India was the main source of diamonds in the world, till in the 18th century, diamonds were discovered in Brazil. But today, very few of the famous diamonds of history taken from the fabulous Golconda mines, are left in India. The Kohinoor adorns the British Crown, the Hope diamond reposes in an American museum and the Orloff and Shah diamonds are secreted in the Kremlin Palace in Russia. It is, therefore, a great achievement for the Indian Government that the largest diamond still left in India today (although African in origin), the 58 faceted, 184.75 carat Jacob diamond, one of the heirlooms of the Nizams of Hyderabad, has finally been acquired for the National Museum at New Delhi for $ 13 million. The Government of India obtained the diamond for the nation at a bargain price. The value at an international auction, in view of its history, would have been at least $ 108 million. For example, the

---

The prices quoted here are in US dollars as the rupee has been devalued in the last hundred years from 40 US cents to less than 3 cents and even more so in terms of actual purchasing power.

much smaller 27.26 carat Chamelon and 21.3 carat Pink diamonds, were sold for $ 7.9 million, by Sotheby's on March 14, 1995, just two months after the Government of India finally obtained the Jacob diamond.

Of the 565 Indian Princely States of the British Raj days, the Nizam of Hyderabad, with domains larger than Great Britain, was the richest and in 1944, the *Reader's Digest* estimated his wealth at over one billion dollars. Even in the early 1950s, after the last Nizam, Mir Osman Ali Khan's efforts to carve a free state outside independent India failed, costing him millions (more than $ 60 million was 'lost' by his efforts to bolster international support), he was still a billionaire. Liquid cash in his personal vaults was estimated at over $ 100 million and jewellery at $ 750 million. This was in addition to real estate worth more than $ 300 million.

By 1956, the shrewd Nizam knew that after his death, all this wealth would be squandered away and so created 27 Trusts to cater to the needs of his descendants and old retainers. Of these, the Nizam's Jewellery

The Nizam — Buyer of the Jacob Diamond

Trust was the richest and in 1972, five years after his death in 1967, at the age of 81, the core of the collection of priceless jewels, totalling 173 pieces, was placed in the vaults of the Hong Kong & Shanghai Bank, in Bombay, for safe custody.

For 23 years the wrangling continued over their value. The whole collection was evaluated by Sotheby's in 1991, at $ 162 million and by Christie's at $ 135 million. In 1995, other experts valued the collection at $ 469 million if sold at international auctions. But, as the items were more than 100 years old, they came under the shadow of the Indian National Heirlooms Act, which prevents national treasures over a century old, being taken out of India and finally, an Arbitrator appointed by the Government of India fixed the price at $ 56 million for the whole treasure, with an additional accumulated interest of $ 9 million for the 23 years delay. The Arbitrator also stipulated that unless the Government of India acquired the treasures for the nation by December 15, 1994, it could be sold to parties outside India by the Nizam's Jewellery Trust. Thus prodded, the Indian Government finally acquired the whole collection.

The collection's piece-de-resistance is the sparkling Jacob diamond, reckoned to be the world's third best in whiteness and seventh in size. Believed to have been found in Africa, this fabulous gem was brought from London to India by a famous jeweller/antique merchant of the last century — A.M. Jacob of Simla. A confidant of Indian maharajas, Jacob (full name Ali Mahommed Yacoub, supposedly a Levantine by birth), was a mysterious figure and has been immortalised in Kipling's novel *Kim*, as Lurgan Sahib of the British Secret Service. The author, Marion Crawford, has also written a novel based on Jacob's life.

But the Jacob diamond proved to be his death knell and the story is interesting. In March 1891, the Nizam of Hyderabad, His Highness Mir Mahbub Ali Khan, asked Jacob to obtain for him a magnificent diamond and after a detailed search, the jeweller located the huge diamond then known as the Imperial. He originally wanted $ 1.84 million, but eventually reduced it to $ 1.6 million. The Nizam wished to inspect the diamond and Jacob respectfully informed the potentate that an advance of $ 1 million would be required before he could hand it over to the Nizam for inspection. Meanwhile, he had a model of the diamond sent to the would-be buyer and the ruler gave him an advance of $ 1 million. The jeweller sent the diamond to the Nizam's treasury and from that day it became known as the Jacob diamond.

But when the news of this purchase reached the British Resident at the Nizam's Court, he was angry with the Indian Prince for spending so much on a 'piece of sparkling vanity'. In those days the British Residents in the Courts of India's native rulers, originally appointed to protect British interests in those particular States, literally ruled Indian royalty. The Resident, Sir Dennis Fitzpatrick, thus went to the Nizam and told him that in the past few years so much money had been spent on jewels that the Hyderabad Treasury was showing a deficit of $ 6 million and with this in view, the British Government would consider adversely any proposal to further increase the debt.

Meanwhile, the British Government in India wrote to the jeweller's firm of Kilburn's, in London, and it was found that Jacob had paid only $ 800,000 for the diamond but was charging the Nizam double his purchase price. On being informed of this, the Nizam was incensed against the jeweller and prevented by his British suzerains from buying the gem, he returned the diamond to Jacob, demanding the deposit back. Jacob, whose financial worth, according to the British Secret Service, was barely $ 320,000, found that he had been saddled with a costly diamond.

Knowing that the Indian maharajas were always keen to

be one up on their peers with regard to the acquisition of priceless treasures, he told the Nizam that the Maharaja of Patiala was eager to buy the bauble. But the Nizam was not moved to buy the diamond in face of the opposition from the British and neither was Patiala. Jacob knew that it was the British Resident at the Nizam's Court, Sir Dennis Fitzpatrick, who was the person behind his problems.

Furthermore, it would have been disastrous for Jacob if it became known that a gem estimated by him to be worth $ 1.6 million, turned out to be only half that value. Anyhow, in a desperate bid, Jacob informed the Nizam that the one million dollars given to him was a security and formed half the price of the gem and that having contracted to buy the treasure, the Indian ruler must follow through on the purchase by paying the rest of the money. He also informed the Nizam that the diamond would not be returned to him unless the balance, more than $ 650,000 was paid.

The furious Nizam instituted a case against the jeweller in the Calcutta High Court, for cheating and criminal misappropriation. One of the star witnesses was Sir Dennis Fitzpatrick. Jacob's advocates wanted to cross examine the Nizam. In British and Indian Jurisprudence, the Indian maharajas, especially the Nizam, could not be sued in any Court unless they themselves voluntarily subjected themselves to its jurisdiction. Although vassals of the British King-Emperor, they were 'independent sovereigns' for the purposes of the Law. It would have been a mortal blow to the Nizam's dignity if he were to divest himself of this immunity and appear as a commoner in a British Court. Therefore, despite the enormous amount involved, the Nizam refused to appear in Court and this legal lacuna, resulted in Jacob being acquitted.

But the implications of the legal battle which cost him $ 160,000 in those halcyon days, ruined Jacob nevertheless, as progressively, many Indian maharajas began to withdraw their patronage from him. Further, the British Government forbade him to enter any of the Indian States. This resulted in many of the maharajas (like His Highness the Maharaja of Dholpur, who owed him $ 125,000) avoiding payment as they could not be sued in any Court.

Finally, Jacob made his peace with the Nizam by persuading the potentate to buy the diamond at a discounted price of $ 240,000. But once the Nizam got the diamond, he refused to pay the balance and Jacob's attempts to obtain the money were in vain. Once, he even succeeded in reaching the Audience Chamber of the Nizam with his appeal, but the documents were thrown in his face by the Nizam's bodyguard. Soon, Jacob found his claim time-barred and the Nizam got the diamond for a comparatively small amount. It is said that later the Nizam took pity on the jeweller and charitably granted him a life annuity of Rs 1000 per month ($ 375 in those days). But to Jacob, who was used to squandering fortunes, this was a mere pittance. He turned blind and died in 1921, a broken man.

But the Nizam did not forget the 'insult' the diamond had brought upon him by being named as a common defendant in a British Court. It is said that out of sheer anger, he kept the diamond in one of his shoes, where it was found when he died in 1911. His son, His Highness Nizam Mir Osman Ali Khan, ascended the throne and the new Nizam had no such prejudices. It is said that he used the Jacob as a paper weight, its shape being that of this mundane stationary item.

A Prime Minister of the Nizam once asked his permission to hold the famous bauble in his hand. But he found the owner's gaze on the diamond so 'drilling', that he hastily handed it back to the ruler.

Loot and chaos reigned in the royal palace of the 81-year-old Nizam Mir Osman Ali Khan, when he died on February 24, 1967 and his 35-year-old successor and grandson, Mir

Barkat Ali Khan, arriving to pay his last respects (and to take over as the future Nizam), found jewel boxes strewn in the hall where the body of the dead potentate had been laid for the public to pay their homage. As the grandson prayed by the side of the coffin, one of the senior-most police officials of Hyderabad came up to him and requested him to take the keys of the jewel safes from the chain suspended around the neck of the dead Nizam before somebody else stole them.

But the Jacob diamond, on account of its rarity, was an unsaleable item in the world jewel market and it escaped the loot. It is one of the most important treasures that the Government of India will put on display in the Indian Jewellery Collection of the National Museum, in New Delhi.

When Mahatma Gandhi Met King George V at Buckingham Palace

In the annals of nations, there are events which though insignificant by themselves, still constitute beacons of national resurgence. For India, the date November 5, 1931, when, during the Round Table Conference, Mahatma Gandhi (clad in his customary dhoti and shawl), walked into Buckingham palace to have tea with King George V, marked a new era in the fortunes of the nation.

More than six decades have passed since that memorable day and both the host and the chief guest have passed into history — but many important onlookers of that famous meeting have left their records of the event and it is possible to reconstruct in detail, the occasion when, as Conservative party journals remarked, the King Emperor took 'tea with Treason'.

It is now known that the British Cabinet at first did not want to associate the King in any way with the Round Table Conference, for it was felt, that if the Conference failed (as it eventually did), it would be bad for the prestige of the Crown. But, at the same time, lack of royal patronage would have made the delegates doubt the bonafides of the British Government and finally it was decided that the King should inaugurate the Conference.

In the first Conference held in 1930, Mahatma Gandhi did not participate, but later his famous meeting with the Viceroy, Lord Irwin, made it possible for him to attend the Round Table Conference of 1931.

But, even as Gandhi decided to go to England, the Conservative diehards in Britain raised their voices against him. Duff Cooper, one such stalwart, remarks in his memoirs that even as early as the 1920s, he had heard Winston Churchill remark that the best fate for Gandhi was to be tied hand and foot and trampled by an elephant carrying the Viceroy of India.

It was, therefore, no wonder that the vituperations of the Tory press against Mahatma Gandhi's visit, ranged from Lord Rothermere's description of the Indian leader as a 'charlatan' to Churchill's tirade against the Viceroy for having allowed the Mahatma to enter the Viceregal palace in New Delhi. Within the Royal family itself, the boycott organised by the Mahatma in 1922, against the Prince of Wales's visit to India, had raised animosity against India's top political captain.

Thus, Lord Irwin, the Viceroy of India, was very much perturbed about this virulent propaganda. He knew that the Mahatma would be meeting the King-Emperor during his stay in England and wanted to keep the King as well disposed towards the Indian leader as possible. Therefore, he wrote on March 13, 1931, a letter to King George V, requesting him not to be prejudiced against the Mahatma.

'I think', the Viceroy wrote, 'that most of the people meeting him would be conscious, as I was conscious of a powerful personality and you cannot help feeling the force of character behind the sharp little eyes ... he affirms that although his aim is that of Purna Swaraj (complete Independence), India will be still requiring British help', and ended with the plea, 'I believe it sir, to be definitely untrue to suggest, as I see it suggested from time to time, that he is out to break the unity of your Majesty's Empire'.

Mahatma Gandhi reached London and the Round Table Conference was in progress. But it was evident from the beginning that it was doomed to failure and a tea-party with the King was arranged as a sop to the delegates. Sir Samuel Hoare, the then Secretary of State for India, confesses in his memoirs that he was very worried about the Mahatma being allowed to enter Buckingham Palace in his 'dhoti and sandals'.

But it was unthinkable to exclude him from the reception and Sir Samuel decided to discuss the matter with the King. When he broached the matter to the King, the monarch turned red with anger. 'What? Have this rebel fakir in the palace, after he has been behind all these attacks on my loyal officers!' he shouted at the Secretary of State.

Later, he subsided to a more even temper, but throughout the discussions regarding the arrangement, he grumbled about having this 'little man in the palace, with no proper clothes on and bare knees'.

But, Sir Samuel Hoare knew that the King had accepted the inevitable and that the Mahatma was to be invited to the function. The invitation was sent to him, but not before some 'discreet whispers' were made to him that it would be better to change his attire into something more formal. But the Indian leader politely insisted that he would wear only his usual dress and the Secretary of State accepted his condition.

On the appointed day, Gandhiji went to Buckingham Palace accompanied by Sarojini Naidu, the eminent nationalist-poetess and his secretary, Mahadev Desai. But it was not the first time that he was meeting the King.

Thirty years earlier, he had met King George V, as Prince of Wales, in South Africa and had presented an address to him on behalf of the Indian community. Then he had been a prosperous lawyer, with an yearly income of Rs 40,000 in those halcyon days. But now, bare headed, clad in his customary loin cloth and shawl, he went to meet the sovereign.

About 500 guests had been invited for the tea-party, including the 89 delegates from India (57 from India, 16 from the Indian States, and 16 from the Government and Opposition members from both Houses of Parliament), as well as the Prince of Wales (the future King Edward VII/Duke of Windsor), who had flown to London from Liverpool to attend the function.

Crowds had gathered outside the Palace, even before the first guest appeared and the weather was fine. Mahatma Gandhi was almost the last guest to arrive and as his car reached the Palace gates, numerous Indians who had come to see him enter the Palace, caught sight of him and waving multicoloured scarfs and handkerchieves, cheered him. As the car passed through the gates, the sentries, by a strange coincidence, came to attention, a honour reserved for royalty alone and never intended for visiting 'fakirs'. Gandhiji smiled faintly as a police constable saluted him and the car reached the portico of the palace.

Most of the other guests had already been presented to the King and Queen and as Gandhi walked up the crimson carpeted staircase, these guests remained close by to see the Mahatma greeting the King and the royal equerries were kept busy imploring the guests not to crowd near the host.

Sir Samuel Hoare, as the Secretary of State, introduced the Mahatma to the King and later remarked that there was a brief difficult moment, as he sensed the King's resentment at having to welcome this guest, who was supposed to be spinning the shroud for the British Raj by his policies. However, the King soon recovered his composure and when their Majesties had shaken hands and greeted all the guests, they went to the reception hall — the Picture Gallery of Buckingham Palace.

There the King mingled with the guests, talking informally with them, while Queen Mary began to converse with the ladies present, especially Sarojini Naidu.

His Majesty first conversed with Sir Akbar Hydari for a few minutes and later moved on to talk to Sir Mirza Ismail, the Dewan of Mysore. Sir Krishnamachari, the Dewan of Baroda was the next delegate to be spoken to and the Mahatma was the fourth guest with whom King George conversed that evening.

The Prince of Wales remarked later that the strangest sight he had witnessed in the Picture Gallery of Buckingham Palace was that of the serried ranks of black morning coated guests parting to reveal the Mahatma in his white dhoti and sandals, advancing to meet the King. The Prince found it hard to believe that scarcely nine years ago, this guest had been imprisoned for sedition.

After the preliminary courtesies, the King remarked to Mahatma Gandhi that he was 'good' when the monarch had met him thirty years earlier in South Africa and that it was only after 1919, that something had gone 'wrong' with him. The Mahatma did not reply to this and maintained a dignified silence. Then the King asked him, 'Mr. Gandhi, why did you boycott the visit of my son to India?' 'No Sir', replied the Mahatma, 'I did not boycott him as your son but as the representative of the British Crown.'

Finally, as the King moved away from his guest, he felt that he must formally warn the Indian rebel-saint against re-starting the Civil Disobedience movement in India. 'Remember Mr. Gandhi, I won't have any attacks on my Empire,' he cautioned the Mahatma and Sir Samuel Hoare, who was standing with them, was afraid that this remark might start an argument between the guest and the host. But the Mahatma's grave and deferential reply, 'I must not be drawn into political argument in your Palace, after receiving Your Majesty's hospitality', saved the day and the King moved on to talk with Sir Tej Bahadur Sapru.

His Majesty had conversed with Mahatma Gandhi for five minutes and the Secretary of State felt that the King's simple sincerity and the Indian leader's beautiful manner made their meeting a success. But he did not fail to notice that the King was occasionally staring with resentment at Mahatma Gandhi's bare knees.

After the conversation, the guests moved on to the Green Dining Room of the Palace for tea. Masses of chrysanthemums and other flowers adorned the Picture Gallery as well as the Green Dining Room and music was played by the string band of the Scots Guards. As the Mahatma took his seat, one of the bejewelled maharajas, whispered to the Prince of Wales, 'This is going to lose you India.'

Mahatma Gandhi did not partake of any of the refreshments and after an hour's stay in the Palace, left for his Knightsbridge residence. Various interpretations and comments have been made about this famous meeting with the King. The Mahatma himself declined to comment on it. Only when one of the reporters queried him about his 'scanty attire', he replied jokingly, 'The King had on enough for both of us'.

But the King's Private Secretary felt that His Majesty had succeeded in warning Gandhi about the consequences of opposing the British Empire. 'His Majesty', wrote the Secretary, Sir Clive Wigram, to the Viceroy of India, 'was, as his custom, very nice to Mr. Gandhi, but ended up by impressing on him that Great Britain would not stand a campaign of terrorism and having their friends shot down in India. His

Majesty warned Gandhi that he was to put a stop to this. Mr. Gandhi spluttered some excuses, but the King told him that he held the Indian leader responsible'.

The pro-British newspapers in India lauded the King for inviting the Mahatma and gently rebuked the Indian leader for his boycott of the Prince of Wales's visit to India, a decade earlier. But as far as the people of India were concerned, they only knew that the uncrowned King of India had met the Crowned King.

The Queen who wanted to be an Empress

The marriage between the Duke of Edinburgh, the second son of Queen Victoria and Princess Marie, the daughter of the Czar of Russia, was one of the most spectacular events of 1874. The wedding took place in St. Petersburg, Russia, on January 23, 1874, and among the galaxy of guests were the Emperors of Prussia and France.

The weeks following the royal couple's return to England were marked by State banquets and receptions and the young Duchess of Edinburgh won the approbation of all by her charm and grace. It was, therefore, a great surprise to the general public, when in March 1874, the Court Circulars revealed that the Duchess would in future abstain from attending Court ceremonies and receptions.

Many reasons were suggested for this decision. The *Times* accounted for it by stating that Her Highness's pregnancy made her retirement from society necessary. But, according to rumours current in Windsor Palace, her absence was due to a quarrel with her mother-in-law, Queen Victoria, over a matter of precedence at Court functions. Subsequently, as events proved themselves, this reason was the correct one.

As the daughter of the Czar, the Duchess of Edinburgh (not unnaturally) thought that she had the right to assume precedence over the Princess of Wales. The children of the Czar were Grand Duchesses and Grand Dukes in their own right and were addressed as Imperial Highnesses. But Alexandra, the Princess of Wales, was only the daughter of a King and was addressed as Her Royal Highness. The Duchess of Edinburgh represented to Queen Victoria that an Imperial Highness must take precedence over a Royal Highness and that she should thus be given the honour accorded to the Princess of Wales in State receptions.

Queen Victoria was considerably embarrassed by this request and tried to impress upon the Duchess the awkwardness of her plea. Even the implication that the British monarchy was inferior to any imperial house of Europe, would be intolerable to the British people, she explained to the Duchess and gently reminded her that the Sovereigns of Great Britain had never admitted that any of the continental Emperors had a title which caused them to take precedence over the King. This reply did not satisfy the Duchess and she informed the Queen of her intention to abstain from Court ceremonies till a mutually satisfactory alternative was found.

Naturally the news reached the Russian capital and Britain heard with interest that the Czar of Russia was about to visit Britain, not merely to visit his daughter but also, if possible, to settle with the Queen the question of precedence that had disturbed her family. Queen Victoria, on her part, was understood to be willing to assent to any solution which did not confer on the wife of her second son the right to take precedence over the consort of the heir apparent. The Czar arrived in England on May 13, 1874 and was received with the utmost cordiality by the Queen at Windsor Palace. The nature of the parley between the Czar and the Queen is not known, but the first effect of his visit was to cause the Duchess of Edinburgh to be described in Court Circulars as 'Her Royal and Imperial Highness, the Duchess of Edinburgh and the Grand Duchess of Russia'. The Czar returned to Russia after a month's sojourn, but the reason for his visit and its implications long rankled in the mind of Queen Victoria.

In Court Circulars, with the exception of the Duchess of Edinburgh, none, not even the Queen was described as Imperial and the Queen decided to take the title of Empress, so that none of her children would be embarrassed at the State receptions of continental Europe, for as scions of an Empress, all of them would be entitled to the prefix 'Imperial Highness'.

The Queen knew well that to be known as the Empress of Great Britain would provoke the animosity of the British people against the throne and to call herself the Empress of Australia or Canada would invite ridicule, as these colonies were then little better than wildernesses. To be the Empress of India, she felt was more suitable, as Emperors were not alien to Indian traditions and scarcely twenty years had passed since the last of the Mughal Emperors had been deposed.

But when she broached the matter to the British Prime Minister Benjamin Disraeli, he was not at all enthusiastic. There had been some question of this in 1858, when India had been brought under the Crown after the Sepoy Mutiny and Disraeli had supported it in principle. But in 1876, the moment was unfavourable. Disraeli knew that this rather un-British idea would be attributed to the Prime Minister's own love for Oriental tinsel, besides he had to obtain the approval of Parliament to have the royal title changed. He requested the Queen to wait for some years, till the atmosphere could be made more congenial for such a Bill to be brought before Parliament. But the Queen was firm in her insistence and the Prime Minister was obliged to accede to her wishes.

Accordingly, while opening Parliament in January 1876, the Queen declared that among the various bills that were to be passed in that session, one would be regarding her assumption of a title 'derived from India'. She judiciously did not mention what the title was to be. The Royal Titles Bill was moved by the Prime Minister in Parliament on February 7, 1876. He had initially thought that it would be against the prerogative of the Crown to state what the new title would be. But most Members objected to this contention and during the second Reading of the Bill, it became apparent that the bill would not be passed unless the new title was disclosed.

Such being the case, the Prime Minister reluctantly made it public that the Queen would be assuming the title of

New Crowns for Old — Times *Cartoon*

'Empress of India'. Parliament was surprised to hear the news and the public outcry was great. The British do not like change. The Queen had always been the Queen. Why should she not continue so? 'The title of Empress', said the puritans, 'evokes images of conquest, of persecution and even of debauchery.' Pamphlets were published as to 'How little Ben, the inn keeper, changed the sign of Queen's Inn to Empress Hotel Ltd. and what was the result?' or 'Dizzi-Ben-Dizzi, the Orphan of Baghdad?'

The foreign embassies found in it a comical story. 'It is the freak of an artist and King-maker in Dizzi', wrote the French *Charge D'affairs*, 'in the Queen the freak of an upstart. She imagines that her standing will be raised and that her children will find a better place for themselves in life with this Imperial title. It is my impression that it is a grave mistake thus to raise the veil, which ought to cover the origin of Crowns. These ought not to be played with. One is born an Emperor and King; but it is very dangerous to become one'.

The Queen was very much grieved by the opposition shown to her wish and especially by the personal attacks her plans had let loose against the Prime Minister. The peers of the House of Lords were as reluctant as the Members of the House of Commons, to sanction the adoption of any exotic title by the Crown. The Crown, on its part, did not scruple to bring to bear personal pressure. Lord Shaftesbury, the most influential of the Peers, was summoned to Court after an interval of twenty-eight years. 'I dread the interview', wrote the aged noble in his diary, 'the cold, the evening dress, the solitude, for I am old and dislike being away from assistance, should I fall ill at night. The Queen sent for me in 1848 to consult me on an important matter. Can it be so now?'

The Queen did not so much as allude to the topic during the interview, but as Lord Shaftesbury shuffled away from the hall, a lord-in-waiting approached him and requested him to convey the Queen's views regarding the matter to his compeers in the House of Lords. But the peer decided to act according to his conscience and on April 3, 1876 moved an address to the Queen in the house of Lords, humbly beseeching her not to take the title of Empress. 'As an Empress, the title has a feminine softness', he appealed, but 'in future, as Emperor, it will have an air, military, despotic, offensive and intolerable.'

It fell to Disraeli's lot to reassure everybody. As regards the negative associations with the name of Empress, he pointed out that the Golden Age of Humanity had been the Era of Antonines. As for the title of the Queen, it would be maintained in Great Britain and in all documents relating to Europe and only in Acts concerning India and in the commission of officers 'who might be called upon to serve India', would the title of 'Empress of India' follow that of 'Defender of Faith'.

Finally, the House of Commons reluctantly agreed to all these assurances, but strangely enough, the House of Lords was more adamant. The Government obtained 137 votes in favour of the title and 91 votes were cast against the bill, including that of Lord Shaftesbury and eight Dukes. Symbolic of public opinion was the comment in the *Saturday Review*, which termed the title a 'vulgar and impolitic appellation'.

The Queen, however, was overjoyed to know the result. When at last she had the title, she wrote to the Prime Minister, a letter of thanks, signing it, 'Victoria Regina et Imperatrix', with childlike delight. Then the new Empress gave a dinner at which she appeared, contrary to her usual custom, bedecked with oriental jewels given to her by the Indian princes. At the end of the repast, Disraeli rose and proposed the health of the Empress of India in a short speech which was crowded with as much imagery as a Persian poem. The Empress responded with a bow that was almost a curtsey. Ironically, her becoming an Empress had not been conveyed to her son, the

Prince of Wales, touring India at the time and he was furious that, despite being the heir apparent, such a decision had been taken without him being informed.

In India, accompanied by salvoes of artillery, the Proclamation of the Queen as Empress of India was made in Delhi, in the presence of the Viceroy and the great feudatories of the Empire, on January 1, 1877. A banner and medal were given to each of the Indian princes to commemorate the event and four of the most important rulers were granted the right to have 21 salvoes fired in their honour during ceremonies, just like the Nizam of Hyderabad. The Viceregal dignity was raised to 31 salvoes. This latter step caused some disappointment among princes like Scindia, who had hitherto been privileged to hold higher rank than the Viceroy in his native dominions and equal rank with him elsewhere, but now found himself deprived of this right.

Ironically, seven decades later, one of the problems involved in the dissolution of the Indian Empire in 1947, was that of the deletion of the British Sovereign's title as the Emperor of India. Although he realised that it was desirable that the title should be shed as early as possible, King George VI tried to preserve it till such time when all the Dominions, as per the Statute of Westminster, had ratified in their Parliaments, this change in the royal title.

But Prime Minister Attlee was adamant and on August 15, 1947, the title of Emperor of India was dropped, although the final Indian Honours List to be published on January 1, 1948, was to be signed as George Rex Imperator, the King's final Act as Emperor of India. This change in the King's title was at once commented on by his mother, Queen Mary, who wrote on the back of the envelope of a letter received from him on August 18, 1947, 'The first time Bertie wrote to me a letter with the letter for the Emperor of India dropped out — very sad'.

Delhi Durbar 1911 — The Grandest Pageant of the Century

More than eight decades ago, the British Empire was at its apex and of all his titles, the one of Emperor of India, appealed to the British monarch most. He especially enjoyed the manner in which he was able to demand the obeisance of the hundreds of Indian maharajas, and the Delhi Durbar of 1911, was the acme of pageantry.

But the organizing of the grand spectacle was a very difficult affair and British officials found the inordinate desire of the Indian prince to rank above his compeer, a great problem. Even sending the invitation required careful vetting and an invitation to the Durbar was to be the proverbial carrot to bring any otherwise reluctant maharajas to Delhi.

In the case of the Nawab of Nawagai, a small chief in the North Western Frontier Province, the main consideration for extending him an invitation was the fact that he had driven out his own son, who was ruining the administration through frivolous policies. For this act of statesmanship, the Nawab was to be rewarded with an invitation. On the other hand, the Maharaja of Karauli wished to expend a lakh of rupees (worth Rs. 8 million in 1995) on his visit to the Durbar. But the Viceroy opined that the small state could not bear this heavy expense and decided to 'excuse' him. In fact, many small rajas, for whom a visit to the Durbar in regal splendour, would have spelled financial ruin, chose the honorable alternative of being 'excused'. For example, the Maharaja of Ajaigarh was given an invitation on the express understanding that he would seek permission to be excused attendance at the Durbar on the ground of financial difficulties.

Originally, it was decided that the amphitheater would provide for 1000 spectators, 150 of the salute princes — Indian rulers entitled to the salute guns occupying the front row. Then it was found that no provision had been made for seating the high dignitaries of the Empire, like the Governors of the different provinces, in the front row and the whole seating programme had to be altered.

Another problem faced by the Durbar Committee was the number of guests/courtiers the different maharajas wished to bring with them. Some of the 21 gun salute States wanted as many as 30 of their premier nobles to be present in the amphitheatre and finally it was decided that the 21 gun salute States would have the right to bring 12 guests each. This number decreased with the number of salutes, with the 'no gun salute' States being permitted only two guests each.

In the desperate race to get one up on their rivals, each maharaja decided to have a larger camp, with a greater number of followers, than his neighbour and the Government of India was forced to warn the rulers that no camp could have more than 500 retainers attached to it. But this was unpalatable to States like Jaipur, which felt that 'though the list of Sardars, officials and followers was most carefully revised and every possible reduction made, yet the number could not by any means be reduced to below 800 — having regard for the pomp and dignity of the occasion and the comfort of the Chief and the Sardars'.

The Maharaja of Patiala wanted some of the best seats in the Durbar for his Spanish wife and her French lady-in-waiting, while the Raja of Jind wanted two seats for his English wife and her daughter. The Viceroy advised his lieutenants that he had no objection to seats being allocated to these 'foreign' maharanis, as long as they were somewhere in the background and not in a prominent position. The British Government had long frowned on these exotic imports and the Viceroy steadfastly refused to meet the foreign maharanis.

But some of the Indian maharanis were not willing to accept the invitation unless they were sure of their 'honoured' place in the hall. In the words of the Governor of Madras, one of the grande dames 'has not yet accepted or declined the invitation and I am convinced, knowing her as I do and from what she told me yesterday, that she is waiting to know whether when at Delhi, her Majesty the Queen will receive the great ladies of India, either separately or at a *purdah* (in private) reception and if so, whether she will be received or will be accorded a seat at the receptions. If the latter, what rank or precedence would she be accorded?' One amusing factor was that the Durbar Committee was asked to provide bolts inside each of the Durbar boxes accommodating ladies, in order to obviate annoyance from inquisitive followers of other ladies.

As regards the noble guests, with reference to one of the Nawabs, there was a sore problem. The British Secret Service had reported that the ruler was suffering from leprosy. Faced with this, the Governor of the State nearest to the ruler's possessions wanted the Viceroy to ban the Nawab attending the Coronation and the Viceroy agreed with his view. But the political Department advised the Viceroy 'that while the Government of India did not want him to attend the Durbar, the objections to his doing so are not sufficiently strong to outweigh the disadvantages of preventing his coming'. Moreover, eminent physicians advised the Viceroy that 'leprosy cannot be said to be either infectious or contagious in ordinary conditions'.

Despite the grand occasion, few of the maharajas succeeded in ensuring that their 'honour' was not compromised by having to bow to the Emperor in Delhi. The Maharana of Udaipur ensured that he did not have to attend the Durbar and the Maharaja of Baroda created a *faux pas* by walking back to his seat after bowing and paying his homage to the Emperor. All the Indian princes, after bowing to their Majesties sitting on the Imperial Thrones on the dais, were to 'retreat' seven steps still facing the throne and then turn to go back to their seats. The Maharaja of Baroda came to the Durbar in a simple outfit of white silk instead of his diamond encrusted Court Dress and viewers felt that he was actually twirling his walking stick as he advanced towards the dais. There he made a cursory bow and walked back to his seat. Aghast at this discourtesy, there was even a proposal to depose him, especially as he had refused to attend a rehearsal which would have shown him how to 'retreat'. Instead, an apology was accepted from him although the imperialist press in India and UK wanted his head.

But the most hilarious incident of the Delhi Durbar was the ease with which one American, Mr. Bryan by name and his wife, managed to gatecrash the function. What transpired was that when Jonathan Bryan and Mrs Bryan of Richmond-Virginia, USA, reached Calcutta in late 1911 in the course of a world tour, they found everybody talking of the Delhi Durbar. Bryan knew the then American President Taft and had a letter of introduction from him to the US Consul in

Calcutta. The 'Durbar mania', with astounding prices being asked for accommodation in Delhi, intrigued Bryan. So, in a mood of speculation, he telegraphed the Secretary of the Durbar Committee, 'Esteem great favour — reserve me two seats have letter from Taft.' But when the telegram reached Delhi, it had an electric effect. For, the name of Bryan was one they were very familiar with, as that of the defeated candidate in the previous American elections. Who knew whether Bryan might not perhaps get elected the next time? And now he wanted to see the British Empire in its full glory ... well ... wheels moved within wheels and to quote Bryan, 'Two days later I was dumbfounded by a call from a railway official saying that a special train would convey myself and Mrs. Bryan from Calcutta to Delhi'.

Now, our Bryan had nothing to do with the defeated candidate in the American Presidential elections ... but why obstruct Dame Luck? To quote a newspaper of the day, 'On arrival in Delhi, he was received by British and Indian officials and with every mark of honour except a military band. He was invited to witness the ceremonies in Court Dress, but having none, he had no alternative but to appear in a plain business suit'. 'We had a special tent', stated Bryan. 'We stood on a carpet of purple and gold within 100 feet of King George and heard every word of the royal speech to the Indian maharajas. I was the solitary individual in civilian dress amidst a vast assemblage of silk and gold lace. I never heard a single unkind comment on my American clothes.'

After the Durbar, Bryan, it must be said in his favour, wanted to pay for the special train and accommodation, expecting to cough up at least $5,000. But to his great pleasure, he discovered 'that an American gentleman armed with a letter from the President of the United States was asked to liquidate no bills at all'. We were even supplied with a special train back to Calcutta. So we saw the Durbar for the price of a telegram from Calcutta to Delhi.'

As the Bryan story appeared in the world press, telegraph lines buzzed from Calcutta to Delhi and a red-faced Durbar Committee denied the whole episode. But a Richmond Yankee in King George's Court had made his mark.

When the Maharana of Udaipur Threatened to Commit Suicide

The first decade of this century saw the British Empire at its zenith. In India, the most precious jewel in the British Crown, the King-Emperor had no vassals more obedient than the 500 odd Indian maharajas, who owed him their wealth and the preservation of antiquated rights to the might of the Imperial Army. The Delhi Durbar of 1911, was held mainly to convey to the Indian princes and peasants the invincibility of the British. In this context it is interesting to record the single instance of one maharaja, the Maharana of Udaipur, who stuck fast to his decision not to attend the grand Durbar, if his pre-eminence among Indian rulers was not recognised.

The Maharanas of Udaipur had always claimed precedence over all other Chiefs in India and in support of their claim, had the valiant saga of centuries of independence from the overlords of Delhi, be they the Mughals or the earlier Moslem Emperors. But in 1911, the proud Rajput ruler was willing to come to the Delhi Durbar and pay homage to the British

Maharana Fateh Singh of Udaipur

King-Emperor, if he was the first potentate to be presented to the suzerain.

This condition the British found difficult to meet as, according to the conventions developed, the Nizam of Hyderabad was to be accorded first place among the Indian satraps. A check of previous occasions when the Maharana of Udaipur visited Delhi, revealed that on no occasion had Udaipur either followed or been preceded by any other Chief in a State ceremony, such as that of a procession or of paying homage. On the other hand, chronicles revealed the great consideration and honours paid by the Mughals to the sons

The Maharana of Udaipur Threatened to Commit Suicide 155

and grandsons of the Udaipur ruler, when the Mughal Emperor had excused the Maharana from personal attendance at his Court and had instead agreed to the Crown Prince of Udaipur coming to the Imperial Court to pay obeisance. The rulers of Udaipur had resented even this concession to Mughal protocol and in order to show that the sending of the Crown Prince to Delhi was the deputation of a very ordinary courtier, had reduced the rank of Crown Prince from that of the 'second Lord in the Kingdom' to that of the 16th grade of courtiers. Ever since those days, the Crown Prince of Udaipur is ranked very low in the protocol of the Udaipur Court, till he succeeds as the Maharana. But the normally sensitive Mughal did not take umbrage at this slight and was pleased that at least the scion of the Udaipur rulers attended his Court.

The British had accepted this supreme position of the Udaipur ruler and in 1832, when Lord William Bentinck, as the Governor General of India, had visited Rajasthan, he stated, 'His Highness the Maharana being lineally descended from one of the greatest families in the country, his rank and dignity have been the highest among the Rajas of Hindustan and will continue to do so.' Further, the British had categorically made it clear to the other Rajput maharajas that Udaipur was their titular doyen ... In 1870, when the Maharaja of Jaipur had declined to attend the Viceroy's Durbar, in case he had to concede precedence to the Maharana of Udaipur, he was asked to leave the Viceregal Camp peremptorily without being accorded any salute or ceremonial honours. As a further measure, the number of gun salutes due to him was reduced. But now in 1911, when the Maharana of Udaipur quoted these precedences, the British informed him that they were willing to make him the highest among the potentates of Rajasthan and that he must follow in the Delhi Durbar, other premier rulers like the Nizam, while paying homage to the King Emperor.

The Maharana disagreed and felt that in case he was not to be the first Chief to be presented to the King Emperor, he should be excused from attendance and be allowed to pay his homage to the suzerain at some other place. The British were surprised at this truculence and warned the Maharana that he would not be permitted to absent himself from the Durbar. The Maharana countered this command by indirectly conveying to the Viceroy that he would rather commit suicide, than follow any other Chief in the imperial procession. This news alarmed the British Government and the Foreign Secretary to the Government of India advised the Viceroy that such a catastrophe would throw an ugly shadow over the whole Durbar and would put more than half the Rajaputana Chiefs into mourning. In any case, the British felt that they would not be able to prevent the Maharana from killing himself, if he decided to take the extreme step.

A frantic check into the annals of the Durbar of 1903, revealed that the Maharana of Udaipur was assigned a place after the five premier States. In fact, the British Viceroy in the 1940s, Lord Wavell, used to humorously memorize the order of precedence amongst the Indian rulers as 'Hot Kippers Make Good Breakfast' (the first letter standing for each of their States), the protocol as Hyderabad first, Kashmir second, Mysore third, Gwalior fourth and Baroda fifth — all 21 gun salute States. Udaipur was only a 19 gun salute ruler. But as things turned out, Udaipur never did occupy second place in the 1903 Durbar, because he never even left his railway saloon after reaching Delhi, having returned to Udaipur immediately. The reason given was his own illness and that of his son, but it was known that these diplomatic illnesses were brought on by the extreme vexation caused by the secondary place given to him for the Durbar.

The British felt that it was of utmost importance to secure the Maharana's attendance at the Delhi Durbar of 1911. He

Heraldic Shield of the Maharana of Udaipur

was again warned that the ceremonial distinctions accorded to him would be annulled and his gun salute would be reduced if he did not pay homage to the King Emperor at the Durbar. But nothing moved the proud Rajput ruler and the British Resident at the Maharana's Court felt that he would indeed commit suicide if coerced, as in the Maharana's opinion — he would rather end his life than allow the pre-eminent position of Udaipur to be damaged in his lifetime.

As the Resident further opined, 'This is a denouement to be avoided at all costs. If one result of the Durbar should be to bring the premier Rajput Chief to grief, this effect would be deplorable throughout India. Whatever punishment may be meted out to Udaipur, we can never dethrone him from his position in the hearts of the Rajput people. If we attempt to do this, we should find ourselves in collision with the Rajputs, the most loyal of all the Indian communities. Jaipur and Jodhpur might fight for the reversion of the premier chief's position, but no one will ever be able to make the Rajputs, as a body, look to any other Chief than Udaipur as their real and natural leader, even though he should be in disgrace with the Sovereign Power.'

Finally, the British felt that they could not take the risk of the Maharana committing suicide and decided to make him a Ruling Chief-in-waiting, a sort of aide-de-camp, so that he would not have to take part as a vassal in the Imperial assembly, but could stand at one side as a dignified companion. But this last minute solution did not appeal to the Maharana and arriving at Delhi, he fell ill, really seriously ill it is said, due to self-administered drugs and apart from taking part in the arrival ceremony at the Red Fort, did not attend the Durbar.

The teams of eminent British physicians and surgeons sent to check on the health of the Maharana found the potentate scarcely able to sit or stand, with large boils in the portion of his anatomy euphemistically known as the backside. Thus, the Maharana retained the proud boast of his clan that they never bowed to the ruler at Delhi, even though he was Sovereign of a quarter of the known world. In fact, it was only in the 1950s, after India attained independence, that the first Prime Minister of India, Pandit Jawaharlal Nehru, persuaded the then Maharana of Udaipur, His Highness Bhagwat Singh, to come to Delhi, no longer as a vassal of any foreign power, but as a citizen of free India and to share with Nehru the podium as a honoured guest in the Republic Day celebrations.

Jawaharlal Nehru and the Maharajas

Historians correctly aver that it was Sardar Patel, who integrated the 565 Indian Princely States into the fabric of the nation, thus ensuring the unity of India. The adroit teamwork of Sardar Patel and the States Secretary, V.P. Menon, is well known in bringing about this great achievement. But, it is not so well known that the initial formation of the States Ministry was to be under Nehru, as the Minister and H.V.R. Iyengar, as the States Secretary. Subsequent developments in the Indian polity and Nehru's pre-occupation with other crucial problems facing India, forced the Cabinet to take the initiative of placing Sardar Patel in charge of the problem of the Princely States.

But, as President of the All India State's People's Conference, Nehru was not a stranger to the problem of the maharajas. Even as a child, he moved in princely circles, as his famous lawyer-father, Pandit Motilal Nehru, was legal adviser to many maharajas. In fact, after the elder Nehru won a difficult court case for him, as a mark of gratitude, one of the rajas suggested to Motilal Nehru that he would settle an annuity of Rs. 500 per month (a princely sum in those days, worth Rs. 40,000 in 1995) in the form of landed property, on Jawaharlal Nehru. But the senior Nehru politely but firmly refused the offer.

While studying in Harrow, the famous public school in Britain, one of Nehru's schoolmates was the crown-prince of Kapurthala. The young prince, used to utmost deference in his native State, did not take kindly to the teasing of his British classmates and used to threaten them, saying that he would have them punished once he became the maharaja. As Nehru points out in his autobiography, this threat did not deter his tormentors and indeed only worsened the situation.

But in India, as Nehru grew in stature as one of the leading lights of the freedom movement and eventually donned the mantle of heir-apparent to the great Mahatma, the maharajas found it difficult to envisage a free India, in which socialist Nehru would be the arbiter of their destinies.

Nehru's secretary, M.O. Mathai, refers to one instance, which shows how correctly Nehru gauged the attitude of the Indian princes towards him. Once, in the British days, while browsing through books in a famous book shop in Simla, the summer capital of India, Nehru found himself tapped on the shoulder by the then Maharaja of Patiala, who had come to buy some books. The Maharaja told Nehru that he wanted to talk to him privately and taking him to a corner, told him that the Indian princes were one with him and the Indian National Congress, in the fight for freedom. But, before they cast their lot with the Congress, they would like to know what the Congress's attitude towards the maharajas would be once freedom was achieved. Before Nehru could essay a reply, the Maharaja told him, 'Think it over and let me know!' and abruptly left the book shop.

Nehru mused over the matter and felt that the Maharaja was not to be trusted. He knew that British spies always followed and kept tag on him and the Indian princes. This meeting, although unplanned, would not have gone unnoticed and the Maharaja would be sure to get a query from the British as to why he was meeting one of the men, who were weaving a shroud for the British Empire. The ruler would then make a 'distorted report of the meeting' to the Indian Political Department.

Nehru wrote a detailed, report of the incident to the Maharaja and ended the letter by asking the ruler what his advice was, so that he, Nehru, could place the proposal before the Mahatma and the Congress Working Committee. Nehru posted this letter by ordinary mail, as he knew that all his correspondence, as well as that of all the Indian princes, was being regularly intercepted by the Government of India. Sure enough, Nehru did not receive any reply from the Maharaja, as he dared not confirm his talk with Nehru. Nehru impishly joked about the Maharaja's consternation when he realised that the Indian Political Department would have got the correct version of his meeting with the Indian leader, from Nehru himself instead of the concocted version to be supplied by himself.

Nehru's record of brushes with the British in the cause of the citizens of Princely States, is impressive. In 1923, he courted imprisonment in Nabha State, in the Punjab, to protest against the ruler's harsh attitude towards the Akali struggle to free the Sikh shrines from interlopers. This led to him being handcuffed and chained to other prisoners. His father, Pandit Motilal Nehru, heard of this from the Viceroy and rushed to Nabha to defend his son, who was by that time stricken with typhoid in the Nabha State prison due to unhygienic conditions and the affair became a *cause celebre*. Finally, Nehru was given a suspended sentence of thirty months of rigorous imprisonment, to be enforced if he entered Nabha State again.

Again, in the months prior to the British Cabinet Mission's

arrival in India in 1945, Nehru courted arrest in Kashmir, protesting against Sheikh Abdullah's imprisonment and Mahatma Gandhi had to intervene before he was released.

In 1945, Nehru, as the President of the All India States People's Conference, declared that the repression in the Indian Princely States was not possible without the Political Department's support. Nevertheless, Nehru was for a friendly approach, urging the rulers to abandon autocracy and where the lack of viability of their principalities was obvious, to merge them with neighbouring provinces. According to Nehru, this would have left about 20 large autonomous states in the Indian Federation, with democratic governments under princely figureheads. (Presidential address to the AISPC, December 31, 1945)

Freedom arrived and during his term as the Vice President of the Interim Government (1946), Nehru participated in many tense occasions of protest against the anti-Indian policy followed by the Political Department of the Government of India. There was even an instance when he threatened to have Sir Conrad Corfield, the Political Advisor to the Viceroy, tried for unlawful exercise of his authority and the destruction of the archives pertaining to the Indian States in the various British Residences in the capitals of the Indian Princely States.

There is evidence to show that the policy making committee of the Indian National Congress and to an extent, Lord Mountbatten too, felt that Nehru's insistence on popular government in the Indian Princely States and his reputation of being a socialist, would come in the way of the Indian maharajas forming a rapport with him.

But Sardar Patel's pragmatic approach in making the princes accede to India on important items like Defence, Foreign Relations, Communications, and Finance while guaranteeing their Privy Purses, with lower priority to adult franchise based on elections in their States, enabled the princes to accept Indian suzerainty more willingly. As is well known, once it was decided that Sardar Patel would be dealing with the princes (except in the case of Kashmir), Nehru scrupulously abstained from interference with the States Ministry, despite being the Prime Minister.

One serious issue regarding the princes on which Nehru held a different view, was the question of Privy Purses being paid to the maharajas 'in perpetuity'. Sardar Patel felt that the Privy Purses agreed upon with the maharajas, as the price for accession, should be guaranteed to them by the Indian Constitution in perpetuity. In fact, Sardar Patel felt so keenly about this point, that despite his being seriously ill in Bombay, he wanted to come to Delhi to sponsor this clause in the Constituent Assembly. Nehru and the Cabinet felt the proposal of 'payment in perpetuity' was unrealistic but in order not to provoke Sardar Patel, postponed the consideration of this clause to a later date. Finally, the commitment was made by the Constituent Assembly in the summer of 1950, when Nehru was away on a State visit to Indonesia.

After Patel's death, Nehru tried through his letters to the major princes in September 1953, to get them to reduce their Privy Purses by a voluntary contribution to the public revenue (of 10 to 15 per cent of the Privy Purses). But he received only evasive replies from the maharajas.

In his personal attitude to the princes, especially after he became Prime Minister of India, Nehru was most considerate and sorted out their individual problems with a sense of historic perspective. In the 1950s, it was he, who persuaded the then Maharana of Mewar, that in view of India being free, the ancient vow of the royal family of Mewar, that they would never set foot in Delhi as vassals, was no longer binding. As a result, the young Maharana came to Delhi as a honoured guest and sat with Nehru at the podium, during the Republic Day celebrations, as a citizen of free India. True to his democratic nature, Nehru did not forget the former subjects of the Maharana, the tribe called Lohars, who had left the historic fort of Chittor after Emperor Akbar conquered it in the late 1590s. The tribe had declared that they would enter Chittor only when it was free of the invaders and under the rule of a sovereign Maharana of Udaipur. Nehru personally talked to them and led them in a joyous march into the ruined fortress as citizens of free India.

Nehru and the Nizam of Hyderabad

Again, when the present Rajmata Gayatri Devi of Jaipur, sought Nehru's help to prevent the demolition of the ancient city walls of Jaipur by the local State Government, Nehru promptly ordered an immediate halt to the destruction. On another occasion, Princess Niloufer (herself the daughter of the last Sultan of Turkey), the daughter-in-law of the Nizam of Hyderabad, complained to Nehru that she was not getting the financial allowances due to her. Nehru 'intervened with the Nizam' and had the allowance restored.

Another delicate 'intervention' Nehru had to perform, was when the Indian Secret Service intercepted the letter written by the Nizam of Hyderabad in early 1948, to his former Suzerain, King George VI of Britain. Aghast at this *faux pas*, the officials sent the letter to Prime Minister Nehru for further action. Nehru realised that such censoring, especially when the letter was for the monarch of Great Britain, was not the 'done thing' and sent the letter to King George VI with an apology, assuring him that he would ensure that such 'mistakes' would not occur again.

At the same time, Nehru was not impressed by the fancy claims of the former rulers. Once, when visiting one of the Nawabs of a central Indian State, as the Prime Minister of India, Nehru was told by the Nawab, that his State was so famous for bravery, that as per legend, once when a tiger pursuing a deer crossed over the State borders, the fleeing deer turned back and attacked the tiger, causing it to turn back. Nehru smiled cynically and told the Nawab, 'Something must be wrong with the tigers in your state...'

Mahatma Gandhi and Adolf Hitler

Mahatma Gandhi had a way of handling the high and mighty. His weapon of non-violence worked with the British. But would it have worked with a tyrant regime like that of Adolf Hitler? There is no need to guess. It is there in black and white for scholars and laymen to see because the confidential papers of the period have been released by India, Britain and Germany — a period which saw the Mahatma (born in 1869) pained by the gruesome World War II unleashed by Hitler (born in 1889).

As Hitler let loose his stormtroopers on Europe, there arose a hope among peace lovers that a towering figure like Mahatma Gandhi could do something to stop the swath of destruction. The fact that the Mahatma was the only world leader advocating non-violence, led to great expectations being pinned on his intervention. How Hitler would have reacted to non-violence is another story. More of it later.

The Mahatma had watched Hitler's rise to power and his subsequent extermination of the Jews. Talking to a group of teachers in 1939, he told them, 'You know what Hitler is doing in Germany. His creed is violence of which he makes no secret.' In another context he addressed an open letter on October 6, 1938, to Czechoslovakia, titled 'If I were a Czech'. In this letter the Mahatma made clear his views on the Munich Pact, known ironically as the 'Peace in Our Time' Pact, by means of which France and Britain handed over Czechoslovakia to Germany.

Mahatma Gandhi said, 'If I have called the agreement with Herr Hitler "Peace without Honour", it was not any reflection on British and French statesmen ... Democracy dreads to spill blood. The philosophy for which the two dictators Hitler and Mussolini stand, calls it cowardice to shrink from carnage.' He advised the Czechs to refuse to obey Hitler and perish unarmed in the attempt. In so doing, he declared, though they would lose their bodies, they would be saving their souls.

The Mahatma had anticipated his well-wishers' retort, 'Hitler knows no pity. Your spiritual efforts will avail nothing

Mahatma Gandhi

before him.' The saint's answer was, 'You may be right. History has no record of a nation having adapted non-violent resistance. Hitherto, he (Hitler) and his kind have built upon their invariable experience that men yield to force. Unarmed men, women and children offering non-violent resistance without any bitterness in them will be a novel experience for them. Who can dare say that it is not in their nature to respond to the higher and finer forces? They have the same soul, that I have!'

Further, the Mahatma expected his sympathisers to twit him saying, 'What you say is all right for you. But how do you expect the Czech people to respond to the novel call? They are trained to fight, in personal bravery they are second to none in the world. For you to ask them to throw away their arms and be trained for non-violent resistance seems to be a vain attempt.'

Mahatma Gandhi's reply to this poser was, 'You may be right ... But I have a call I must answer ... This is how I should, I believe, act if I was a Czech.' As the skirmish developed into a full-fledged invasion of Poland by Germany, the Mahatma wrote bitterly, 'Germany is showing to the world how efficiently violence can be worked, when it is not hampered by any hypocrisy or weakness, masquerading as humanitarianism'.

The Mahatma found it becoming increasingly difficult to brush aside requests from his followers all over the world to do something. So he decided to write to the priest of violence and on July 23, 1939, penned the following letter to Hitler. 'Dear Friend', the letter began, 'Friends have been urging me to write to you for the sake of humanity. But I have resisted their request, because of a feeling, that any letter from me would be an impertinence. Something tells me that I must not calculate and I must make my appeal for whatever it may be worth.

It is quite clear that you are today the one person in the world who can prevent a war which may reduce humanity to the savage state. Must you pay that price for an object, however worthy it may appear to you to be? Will you listen to the appeal of one who has deliberately shunned the method of war with considerable success? Anyway I anticipate your forgiveness, if I have erred in writing to you.'

The letter was sent to the Government of India for forwarding to Hitler but the Viceroy of India refused to send it with the result that only the nationalist newspapers in India and some British journals carried the Mahatma's exhortation.

The letter evoked widespread comment but this was mostly sceptical. While some admirers of the Mahatma applauded his stand, by and large world opinion felt that the Mahatma was impractical. It echoed the views of the American missionary who, earlier in 1938, had berated the Mahatma. 'You do not know Hitler and Mussolini', he had told the apostle of non-violence during a meeting and added, 'They have no conscience and they have made themselves impervious to world opinion. Would it not be playing into the hands of these dictators, if, for instance, the Czechs following your advice confronted them with non-violence. Seeing that dictatorships are immoral by definition, would the law of moral conversion hold good in their case?'

Apart from this, there was ample evidence of how Hitler would respond. Talking to Lord Halifax (who as Lord Irwin, the former Viceroy of India, had negotiated with the Mahatma), Hitler had berated the British statesman in 1937, for permitting the Mahatma and the Indian National Congress to parley with their 'British Masters'. 'Shoot Gandhi and if that does not suffice, go on shooting down all the other leaders, till they realise that you mean business and that would stop their agitation', was Hitler's 'considered' advice.

Mahatma Gandhi's anguish increased as World War II

Adolf Hitler

raged on and the detractors of non-violence increased in number. He was forced to say defensively, 'How do we know for whose destruction Hitler was born?' Again he penned a letter to Adolf Hitler on December 24, 1940, stating, 'That I address you as a friend is no formality. I know no foes. My business in life has been for the past thirty-three years to enlist the friendship of the whole of humanity by befriending mankind, irrespective of race, colour or creed. I hope you will have the time and desire to know how a good portion of humanity, who have been living under influence of that doctrine of universal friendship (viz: non violence) view your action.'

After imploring him to adopt non-violence, the Mahatma pleaded, 'I therefore appeal to you in the name of humanity to stop the War'. In the last paragraph of the letter, the

Mahatma added, 'This letter is addressed to Mussolini also, whom I met in Rome'. But with the war on, the Government of India decided not to allow this letter to appear in the Indian newspapers, classifying it as an anti-war effort. The letter was returned to the Mahatma with the censor's regrets. Gandhi could have easily had it published in the nationalist journals. But as he wrote to the Viceroy, 'I do not want surreptitious publication'.

It is a measure of Mahatma Gandhi's greatness that he applied the same yardstick to his colleagues in the Indian freedom struggle, when they became Ministers of the Indian Government overnight in 1947. He did not spare them for forsaking non-violence. In an interview with the journalist Kingsley Martin, on January 27, 1948, one finds the Mahatma intensely disillusioned. He confessed that he now realised that the non-violence practised by the Indian masses was simply a 'non-violence' of people who had no military strength. He had witnessed it in 1946 in the communal riots in Bengal. He was aware that the freedom struggle in India had not been a non-violence movement in the highest sense of the term.

It was the same in the case of Kashmir, where the new Government of India had to use military strength to repel Pakistani raiders. The members of the Indian Cabinet did not seek recourse in non-violence, a remedy the Mahatma had advised Hitler to pursue. Ruefully, the saint recalled what Maulana Azad, one of his foremost disciples (a Cabinet Minister of the Indian Government in 1948) had once said, 'When we gain power, we shall not be able to hold it non-violently'.

Thus, bitter that his own disciples had forsaken him, three days later, on January 30, 1948, the apostle of non-violence fell a prey to violence.

A Portion of India That Will Always be Burma

One of the tragedies of the 19th century for some of the Asian nations, was the manner in which the British played with the lifes and fortunes of the scions of the ancient ruling dynasties of the East. Prominent among them were Emperor Bahadur Shah, the last of the Mughals and King Theebaw of Burma. Strangely enough, the Indian potentate was sent to the city of Rangoon in Burma to spend his years of exile, while the deposed Burmese ruler was kept as a prisoner-guest in the town of Ratnagiri in western India.

It is pointless to debate now the reasons why King Theebaw failed as a ruler and had to surrender his country to the British. He was a 26-year-old monarch surrounded by crafty courtiers, when the British took over Burma in 1885. But Theebaw's character has been cleared of many of the malicious allegations the British circulated about him. Even conservative British historians have conceded that Theebaw was not the decadent drunkard that the foreign Press (mainly

A Portion of India That Will Always be Burma 173

British), described him to be. But, he was a much weaker ruler than his father who had skilfully parried the British for 25 years.

Theebaw's attempt to counter balance British aggression by inviting the French to establish commercial interests in Burma, only hastened the evil day and the Viceroy of India gave him an ultimatum in November 1885, that he should either agree to become a feudatory of the British Empire like the Indian Princes or face the British Army. Theebaw called upon his people to fight 'the heretics, the British barbarians'. But within a month, the British forces captured Mandalay — the Burmese capital. Forced to surrender himself and his family to the British, Theebaw was immediately exiled to India. He later claimed that jewels and treasures worth millions of rupees were left with the British Commandant for safety and that none of these were returned to him. The list included among other regalia, 24 sets of diamond necklaces and 10 diamond chains, besides the priceless Crown ruby *Ngamauk*. It was thereafter discovered that most of the treasures had been looted and the rest credited to the Prize Committee of the British Army, the British Regalia and to museums in Britain. Even so when he left shores of Burma, Theebaw and his queens managed to retain treasures worth seven lakhs of rupees conservatively.

Here are abstracts from the records kept in the National Archives of India of the *Ngamauk* — the fabulous ruby alleged to have been lost by the ex-King Theebaw of Burma.

The Mogok rubies of Burma enjoyed the same fame in history as the diamonds of Golconda in India. It is not so well known that the most famous ruby in the world — a veritable Kohinoor among rubies, the *Ngamauk*, was lost from the treasure chest of King Theebaw of Burma in 1886 and has not been heard of so far. It is presumed that it is with the family of some of the British soldiers, who looted Theebaw's palace on that fateful day in 1886.

The famous ruby was set in a ring and was known as the *Chindwin Ngamauk* or simply, *Ngamauk*. It was a priceless stone of unequalled brilliance, having been among the Burmese Regalia for centuries, since the days of King Bodawpaya and tradition decreed that as long as the rulers of Burma had this famous ruby with them, they would remain suzerains of Burma.

After the defeat of King Theebaw in 1886, British forces under General Prendergast entered Ava — the royal citadel, and a battalion under the direct orders of Colonel Sladen (Later Sir Edward Sladen), entered the royal palace. When queried 25 years later by the British Government, Sir Sladen stated that on entering the palace, he saw the King and the Queen with some of the Ministers at the Audience Chambers, with the Regalia and other valuables consisting for the most part of large and small utensils of gold, some of them studded with precious stones. They all lay in heaps on the floor of the verandah. There was no attempt to hand over particular items or a given quantity of anything: The King and Queen at the time were in great grief and trepidation. The palace was being overrun by numbers of common women, who were looting in all directions and carrying away bundles and boxes from the royal apartments, under the eyes of the King and the Queen. 'It was only when I realised the great value of the property and the danger it was in of being immediately removed, I slipped away alone and came back to the royal apartments with a guard composed of officers.'

It is not known what happened after Colonel Sladen returned with his officers-guard. One year later, King Theebaw, from his exile in far-off Ratnagiri, in the then Bombay Presidency of India, wrote to the British Government that the famous *Ngamauk* ruby ring and a great portion of his private diamonds, had been given by him to Colonel

Sladen for safe custody and that Colonel Sladen had given the undertaking that the deposed King would get back the Crown and State property. But after his exile to India, these precious treasures were not returned to him and he wanted the British Government to honour its commitments. But no action was taken and it was only 25 years later in 1912, when the King, having disposed of the few treasures he had brought with him, made another appeal, that the British Government decided to investigate the matter.

Colonel Sladen vehemently denied knowledge of any undertakings given to King Theebaw and stated, 'When I returned with the guard, I found that the King and the Queen had left the palace and returned to a summer house in the adjoining garden. Their attendants were busy removing the royal baggage, consisting of numerous boxes and bundles from the palace; no one was really in charge of the property at this time and it is impossible to say whether any or what portion of the Regalia may have been carried away with the royal effects or during the previous night when most of the minor queens and princesses fled the palace, with some 300 maids of honor! A good deal of valuable portable property would have assuredly accompanied them. The more bulky articles, which came into my possession or which I may say I rescued from being carried away altogether, I then and there made over to a military guard and on the same day, before Theebaw was led away as a State prisoner. I took General Prendergast to the spot and pointed out the arrangements made for the protection of this particular property. A Committee was at once appointed to take charge of all palace property and my responsibilities ceased. I did not belong to this Committee and had nothing whatever to say as to its operations and proceedings beyond occasionally putting it in the way of recovering Royal property, including timber, elephants, ponies and so on. I was present for a portion of the time, whilst the Regalia was being packed away by the Committee into large packing cases. Soldiers and sailors were employed to pack, but I do not think any list of contents were made at this time. There was far too great confusion to admit of more being done than securing as much as could be safely put away in a rough and ready sort of way, with the prospect of preparing detailed lists at a more convenient season, as soon as matters settled down and a fixed administration had been established.'

An investigation into ex-King Theebaw's memorial showed that in 1886, some jewels were recovered from him and sent to Her Majesty Queen Victoria. They included Theebaw's best Crown, three emeralds from Theebaw's second Crown, an envelope containing light loose stones, which had dropped out of the Crowns and a necklace with a diamond peacock and a gold comb. The rest of the jewels were housed in the South Kensington Museum.

One of the Burmese monks, known as Shwedaik Atwinun, was present during the listing of King Theebaw's jewels by Colonel Sladen and Colonel Sladen never denied the presence of this dignitary. But he refuted the allegation that any formal list was made.

More than King Theebaw, his consort Queen Supayalat, felt with her woman's sense of tradition, the loss of the famous ruby and very frequently urged her husband to press the British King for its restoration. But always the reply was, 'His Majesty the King has not been pleased to issue any commands thereon.'

(A ruby called the Theebaw ruby, of 24.82 carats, appeared in the market in 1937 and decades later, was bought by Van Cleef and Arpels on May 27, 1971. It is not known as to whether it is the same as the *Ngamauk*).

King Theebaw died in 1916, but many of his ex-officers were alive till recently and we are able to reconstruct the last days of the monarch. Prominent among these officers was the late Rao Bahadur K.R. Shitut, who besides officiating as the Dewan (prime minister) of Theebaw, was the chief minister of many smaller Indian Princely States. I had the good fortune to discuss with Mr. Shitut, his days with the former Burmese monarch.

Initially the ex-King was kept at Madras for a few months, as his chief Queen Supalayat, was expecting a child. When the baby was born, Theebaw ordered a gold platter three feet in diameter and studded with rubies, for the naming ceremonies. On April 16, 1886, the refugees landed at Ratnagiri, on the west coast of India, where two large houses had been prepared for them. Theebaw spent 30 years in Ratnagiri and his last days were passed in a new mansion (at present known as Theebaw's Palace), built for him in 1910. This double-storeyed house with 15 living rooms, a Durbar Hall and outhouses for 60 servants, was built at a cost of 1¼ lakhs of rupees (nearly £10,000). This huge establishment, which numbered 161 members, proved a huge drain on his allowance. Even otherwise, the ex-King had not managed his treasures carefully and according to the late Mr. Shitut, squandered away all his jewels within a decade of his arrival in Ratnagiri, mostly to avaricious moneylenders. The eminent historian, W.H. Desai, quoted an instance when a jewel worth more than 2 lakhs of rupees was sold for less than 40,000 rupees. The establishment charges for King Theebaw were to be limited to Rs 46,794 per annum. Despite this, towards the end of the 19th century, the Government of India was forced to pass a law 'incapacitating Theebaw from binding himself by contract', so that no moneylender could cheat him. A committee was appointed to manage his wealth and allowance and finally, when Theebaw died, necessitating his family's return to Burma, Rs 39,000 was held in trust for them.

There is no doubt that the former monarch, because of his confinement in the remote township of Ratnagiri, was forced to while away his time in idleness for three decades, writing appeal after appeal to the British, to ameliorate his lot. He even tried to meet King George V, when the monarch came to India for the Delhi Durbar in 1911. But his request was not granted. His Chief Queen, Supalayat, was a lady who never forgave the British nor forgot that she was once the Queen of Burma and tried to maintain the immediate circles surrounding her and her husband, in the manner of a miniature court. Menials had to crawl on all fours when approaching the King and for decades, the first thing the Queen did in the morning, was to crawl before Theebaw with offerings of flowers, after which she was allowed to stand or sit as he desired.

The enforced absence from Burma, cut off from the cultural life of which he was head, created many problems for Theebaw, with no eligible princes to marry his daughters (there were four of them). The princesses contracted alliances with commoners instead. The first daughter, known as the First Princess, had an affair with the gatekeeper of the mansion and his second daughter, eloped with Theebaw's private secretary- a Burmese. Born to the purple as he was, Theebaw mourned his second daughter's misdeed in marrying a Burmese of lowly rank, more than the first daughter's carrying on with the Indian servant, a foreigner. In the words of historian W.H. Desai, 'When Theebaw saw the carriage returning empty without his daughter, he had a heart attack and died about the midnight of December 16, 1916'.

His mortal remains were enshrined on March 21, 1919, in a tomb built in Ratnagiri. His family wished to carry back his embalmed body with them to Burma. But the British Government felt that his remains would become a rallying point for the Burmese nationalists and refused the request.

Queen Supalayat and her daughters left Indian shores in April 1919 and when she died in 1925 at Rangoon, the resurgent Burmese nationalists honoured her with a magnificent funeral, as though she were still the Queen of Burma. Today, a number of King Theebaw's descendants work as menials and petty shop keepers in Ratnagiri. His former residence was for some time the District Collector's residence-office. Later, it was converted into a polytechnic for local students. In 1948, when Burma became free, the Government of independent India returned all available treasures of Theebaw to Burma, including his magnificent wooden throne, which had been kept in an Indian museum.

But the memory of the hapless 'Theebaw Raja', as he was known in Ratnagiri, will always remain and by the sea-girt shores of Ratnagiri, King Theebaw's tomb will be 'a little portion of India that would always be Burma'.

Muslin — The Fabric that Ruined its Weavers

In the history of fabrics there is no name more famous than that of Dacca muslin. Even today, among aristocratic families of the Indian subcontinent, old pieces of Dacca muslin are still considered the ultimate in luxury textiles. In the first decades of the 20th century, one than (one yard wide, ten yards long) of muslin, known as Shama or Evening Dew, cost Rs. 400 or Rs 40 per yard. It would be worth Rs 12,000 per yard in today's inflationary times.

The word 'muslin' derived from the name of the city of its origin, Mosul, in Iraq and through the centuries when India became known as the home of exotic muslins, two Indian cities, namely Masulipatnam in south India and Dacca, in Bengal, became famous for the weaving of this cloth.

There are many fabulous stories connected with Dacca muslin. Their weave was so fine that the Egyptian Pharaohs used them for wrapping mummies. Pliny, the famous Roman historian, refers to one type of Indian muslin known as Jhuna, worn by Roman ladies of high rank, to show off the contours of their bodies. The variety known as Sarkar-e-Ala, was used for the turbans of the Mughal Emperors. Imperial Rome imported large quantities of this fabric, with embroideries done in silver or with silk thread and these muslins were known as Kasidah. The history of Dacca muslins is replete with exotic names like the varieties of Kasidah known as, Qutn-e-Rumi, Naubati, Yahudi, Alizolah and Samanderlaher.

Till 1813, Dacca muslin continued to sell in London with 75 per cent profit and was still less costly than the local British make. Alarmed at this exotic competition, the British imposed 80 per cent duty on this Indian product. But more than the duty, the introduction of machine-made yarn, ruined the industry, as by 1817, English mill-made thread was introduced in Dacca, at one fourth the price of Indian yarn. Till 1821, one of the main problems faced by the Dacca weavers was to go around collecting yarn from the local spinners. This yarn was not of a uniform quality. But, with British machinery,

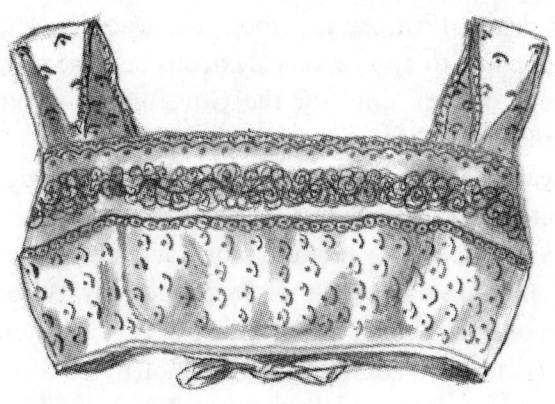

Muslin Embroidered with Silver Wire

yarn of a uniform texture could be obtained and soon the Indian handmade yarn industry closed down.

In 1840, Dr Taylor, a British textile expert wrote, 'Even in the present day, not withstanding the great perfection which the weaving art has attained, the Dacca fabrics are unrivalled in transparency, beauty and delicacy of texture and excel the most finished product of the looms of any country in the world'. The count for the best variety of Dacca muslin, was 1800 threads per inch, while the lesser varieties were 1400 threads per inch.

Another unsavoury fact associated with the killing of this Indian industry, was that many expert yarn makers of Dacca had their thumbs and index fingers chopped off by the British in order to prevent them from twisting the finer yarns required for the muslins.

Despite producing the costliest fabric in the world, the weavers of Dacca were ruined by their skill. During Mughal days, the finest muslins of Dacca were reserved for the Imperial Court. The most famous of the weavers were registered as though in royal employ and were not allowed to make muslins for any others. The traveller, Above Rynal, remarked in the 17th century about the Dacca weavers, 'It was a misfortune to appear very dextrous because they were then forced to work only for the Government which paid them ill and kept them in a sort of captivity'.

The weavers were paid so little that, during the era when a rupee fetched 2 1/2 maunds of rice, they got only 1 to 1 1/2 rupees per month. By modern monetary value, this would mean a maximum daily wage of Rs 50 per day. Among the aristocrats of north India, till a century ago, mill-made cloth was abhored and only muslin was good enough for daily wear.

In 1875, when Edward VII, the then Prince of Wales came to Bengal, Sir Abdul Gani of Dacca, had ordered 30 yards of the most superior muslin as his gift to the Prince. One yard of this fabric weighed barely 10 grams!

Washing, pressing and polishing the muslin was one of the specialised tasks of Dacca's washermen community. An interesting fact was that the polishing of muslin was done using conch shells and the fabric was not ironed. The best test of the material was that repeated washing made it finer. So specialised was this laundrying of muslin, that the *Ain-E-Akbari* or the chronicle of the Mughal Emperor Akbar's era, mentions that only the water of the Khasnagar tank near Dacca had the special quality required to bring out the best in the muslin. Safflower and indigo were the main dyes used for imparting colour to this fabric.

Dr. Taylor states, 'Hindu women of the age, varying from 18 to 30 years, were the weavers of superfine quality. But after 30 years, their sight became impaired. The superfine quality could be woven only in early morning or afternoon as otherwise the strong sunlight snaps the threads.'

Unlike the case of many famous handicrafts of the subcontinent, which were revived by the Government of India after independence, till Bangladesh became a sovereign nation in 1971, there was not much attention paid to the development of the Dacca muslin industry, although on a commercial scale, the manufacture of Kasidah and Jamdani fabrics continued. After 1971, the Bangladesh Government and the West Bengal State Government in India, have tried to revive muslin weaving and the few samples that have come into the market, leads one to believe that the glorious days of the Dacca muslin might return!

They Wanted to Build Another Taj Mahal

Probably more encomiums have been showered on the Taj Mahal than on any other edifice created by man. It has often been debated whether it is possible to build an edifice more magnificent than the Taj Mahal.

Thus far the challenge has remained unanswered, although many noteworthy attempts have been made to build a monument equalling, if not excelling, the grand mausoleum at Agra. Strangely enough, the first such attempt was made by none other than the Emperor Shah Jahan himself, whose love for his Empress Arjmand Banu Begam (the official name of the Lady of the Taj, Mumtaz Mahal) resulted in the creation of the Taj Mahal. Having built the Taj Mahal, the Emperor felt that it would be befitting to have another mausoleum, the exact replica of the Taj, but in black marble, constructed on the opposite bank of the river Jamuna, which would house his mortal remains.

He further decided to have a marble bridge built across the Jamuna to connect these two mausoleums so that, as in life, he and his beloved would remain united in death also.

On completion of the Taj, Shah Jahan ordered the master

builder to start work on the Black Taj Mahal. But it is doubtful whether even Shah Jahan, the richest of the Mughal Emperors, could have financed the building of the Black Taj Mahal.

In building the Taj Mahal, the Mughal treasury shouldered

Black Taj Mahal & White Taj Mahal

only one third of the expenses, the rest being borne by 'contributions' or 'offerings' from the maharajas and nawabs, vassals of the Mughal Empire. Further, the cost of the superior Caucasian black marble to be used in the Taj, was five times that of the pure white marble used from the quarries of India. Tradition avers that while building the Taj Mahal, Ustad Isa, the master architect, ran short of black marble and was forced to use white marble soaked in certain chemicals for years, till it acquired the proper black colouring. The expense of building the Black Taj Mahal would have been, at least, Rs 25 million, compared to Rs 5 million spent on the Taj Mahal.

One must remember that in terms of purchasing power, one rupee in the 17th century, was worth 412 times more than the 1992 rupee — or the Black Taj Mahal would have cost more than 10 billion rupees (£350,000,000).

Anyhow, the fratricidal wars that ravaged the Empire of Shah Jahan during his last years, put an end to the grand scheme. Today, on the bank of the Jamuna, opposite the Taj Mahal, one merely sees the vast red sandstone platform that was to be the foundation of this mausoleum.

ShahJahan and Mumtaz Mahal

Aurangzeb, Shah Jahan's successor, was not interested in completing the monument and when Shah Jahan died, his remains were placed in the same crypt as Mumtaz Mahal. 'The mortal remains of my parents should lie buried side by side, as they loved each other so strongly', Aurangzeb decided, 'but to build another such monument would be wasteful and ridiculous excess.'

It therefore seems somewhat ironical, that the second attempt to build another Taj was made by the Emperor Aurangzeb himself. This time, it was in memory of his wife, Dilras Banu, surnamed Rabia-ud-Durani and better known as Durani Begum.

She died in Aurangabad, in south India and the edifice known as Bibi-ka-Muqbara, is the mausoleum Aurangzeb erected as her memorial. This mausoleum cost him Rs 7 lakhs (£10,000,000 in 1992) and took seven years to build. Chronicles mention that the marble had to be brought from north Indian quarries and that master architects, Ataulla and Haibat Rai, designed the monument.

But to any observer, it becomes apparent that this monument (built within seven years of the completion of the immortal Taj), while following in outline the basic features of the Agra edifice, is no equal to it. According to the well-known art historian, Percy Brown, Bibi-ka-Muqbara falls far short of the Taj in that the symmetry and the simplicity are absent in it.

The mausoleum is approached by a paved avenue. There is a wide pond with 12 fountains in its centre. At the end of the avenue, within a spacious area, stands the monument. The total height of the edifice is 110 ft above ground level. Up to a height of five ft from the terrace, the building is of pure marble and above this height, the superstructure is of stone stucco. On the top, the huge dome is again of white marble.

The decline of the Mughal Empire and the distance of Bibi-ka-Muqbara from the Imperial capital of Delhi, caused the edifice to fall into disrepair and Aurangzeb's son, Prince Azam, rebuilt it again.

The centuries that followed spelt ruin for this monument and the costly treasures inside it. At the beginning of the 20th century, Lord Curzon ordered the cataloguing and conservation of the old chinese porcelain, copperware and carpets that had been lying neglected in the tomb. Since then, the Government of India has spent a lot of money in the upkeep of the monument.

Lord Curzon, the Viceroy of India (1896-1906), took a keen interest in the architectural heritage of India and the Indian Archaeological Department owes its present status to this illustrious Viceroy. 'It was Lord Curzon, who made a positive attempt to find the fate of the Peacock Throne, another master creation of Emperor Shah Jahan and thanks to his efforts, the historic monuments of Agra, including the Taj, have been saved from the ravages of time', as quoted by his biographer Lord Ronald Shay.

But this Viceroy had a greater ambition to fulfill. This was to build in India, an edifice to perpetuate the memory of Queen Victoria, 'just like the Taj Mahal was meant to keep immortal the memory of the Queen of Shah Jahan'.

The third attempt to raise an edifice to equal the Taj was thus made by Lord Curzon and this resulted in the building of the Victoria Memorial, known as the 'Twentieth Century Taj', in Calcutta.

When the news of the death of Queen Victoria reached him, a Committee was set up by Lord Curzon to build a stately building, which in its shimmering beauty would be a worthy rival to the Taj in Agra.

'I want a magnificent shell', Lord Curzon wrote to the architect, Sir William Emerson, 'pure and severe in its simplicity, with various galleries and corridors radiating around its centre space, which will be devoted to the Queen.' As it happened, the architect chose the Italian Renaissance style for the Victoria Memorial Hall.

Today, the 183 ft high Victoria Memorial (costing Rs 7.2 million in 1921, equivalent to £70 million in 1992), is one of the most magnificent buildings in India and houses a priceless collection of paintings and antiques, including one by the Russian artist Verestagin, reputed to be the second largest painting in the world.

Over the centuries, in different parts of India and even in Europe, admirers of the Taj have built miniature Taj Mahals as mausoleums for their beloved dead. In Agra, the city of the Taj itself, the old Roman Catholic cemetery contains a miniature Taj Mahal built by Colonel Jon Hessing in 1800 AD on the demise of his wife Alice. In Lucknow, the former capital of the Nawabs of Oudh, the compound of the *Chota Imambara* contains an exquisite model of the Taj Mahal as a part of the religious complex. In far off Europe, in Paris, one of the local cemetries contains a miniature Taj Mahal, a memorial to an Indian Muslim noble, who died in France in the 19th century.

The current attempt to build an edifice equalling the Taj Mahal, which stands in the city of Agra itself, is by the Radhasoami Sect of Hindus in memory of their founder, who died in 1878 and 'when completed, the memorial will rival the Taj'. The work has been in progress since 1904 and is estimated to require 350,000 square feet of best quality marble and according to the architect in charge, only a fraction of the edifice has been built so far. To carve manually a piece of marble three ft long, takes a very long time and one of the carvings took eight years to complete. Totally shunning mechanical implements, all carvings are carried out by families of the famous marble carvers of Agra and often one finds three generations of craftsmen working on a piece of marble.

The memorial is to be completed, hopefully, within the next five decades and a model of the building as it will appear when completed, is displayed in the halls of the Radhasoami Memorial Society.

The building has an oriental setting, but different styles have been beautifully combined. The original estimate of the expense was Rs 5 million. But it is opined by the builders, that when completed, the cost may be as high as Rs 1,000 million. The total height of the Memorial will be 193 ft and ten inches, 16 ft less than the height of the Taj Mahal.

On ascending to the top of the incomplete second floor one can see the Taj, resplendent in the far off horizon. But will the Radhasoami Memorial excel the Taj Mahal?

Danish Castle on Indian Shores

Today, Tranquebar is a small town with a population of barely 4,000 and hardly a hundred houses, located on the eastern coast of India, 300 km south of the metropolis of Madras. The local industry consists of fishing and salt-panning. Yet, but for a small twist of history, Tranquebar, known as Tharangambaddy (meaning in the local Tamil, 'village with dancing waves'), might have become another grand metropolis like Madras, Calcutta or Bombay or at least another Pondicherry, the nearby former capital of French India. For it was at Tranquebar, on October 11, 1620, that a Danish fleet arrived to pursue the ambition of King Christian IV of Denmark, to establish an empire in India. The Danish fleet was commanded by Admiral Ove Gedde.

This relatively unknown saga of Danish efforts to build an empire rivalling the British and French, makes interesting reading. Denmark's ambitious King Christian IV, in 1619 felt that the time had come to build a Danish Empire and taking advantage of a mission from the King of Ceylon to Europe, asking for help against the Portuguese, sent a fleet under Admiral Ove Gedde. Reaching Kandy, the Ceylonese capital,

Ove Gedde found that the Portugese had defeated the Ceylonese army. Local Danish settlers informed him that Raghunatha Nayak, the king of Thanjavur, in nearby south India was favourably inclined towards the Danes. So, on October 11, 1620, the Danes landed at the seashore village of Tranquebar.

The Thanjavur king gave the village to his new friends and the five-mile-long, three-mile-broad Danish settlement became part of Indo-Danish history. The Danes had to pay an annual tax of Rs 3,100 to the Thanjavur king.

Within two months, Ove Gedde started building a fort and today, the Dansborg is the only reminder left of Danish dreams of an Indian Empire. As per the guide book of Tranquebar published by the Lutheran Evangelical Church of south India by historian Rev. Gruendler, 'The original shape of the fort designed according to contemporary European rules of fortification, has been fairly well preserved through the 380 years of its existence. It consists of a square inner courtyard surrounded by buildings on all sides and enclosed by brick walls which in the corners widen to protecting bastions.'

The original Dansborg had in addition to the walls, a moat which was connected with the river to the south of Tranquebar. The main gate, which today opens directly towards the former parade ground, could only be entered after passing over a drawbridge. The Dansborg, though designed as a self-contained fort, was also meant to be the cornerstone of a system of defences enclosing the whole town of Tranquebar, constituted by a high brick wall with protruding bastions. In the early 18th century, there were six bastions facing the land — Prince George, Golden Lion, Norway, Holstein, Klingenborg and Laland. But the defences of Tranquebar were never tested in battle. In 1801 and 1807, when the British threatened invasion, the Danish Governor surrendered rather than risk destruction.

Although in the early 19th century, the defences were strengthened, the vanishing fortunes of Denmark as a colonial power made it unnecessary for Tranquebar to be defended. After 1845, when the whole colony was sold to the British for Rs 12.5 lakhs or about £100,000, all the guns were disposed off as ballast for ships.

Although militarily Tranquebar was not famous, historically it ranks with Goa on the west coast, Kerala to the south and Serampore in Bengal, as one of the four cradles of Christianity in India. In fact, it was at Tranquebar that the first Protestant Church was built in 1671. The arrival of Bartholomew Ziegenbalg, on July 7, 1706, was a landmark in the annals of Indian Christianity. Till today, Tranquebar derives its importance from the activities of Christian missionaries.

From old maps of the small town, it is clear that it must once have been a flourishing centre and even today street names such as Prince Christian Street, Admiral Street and Queen's Street, bring to mind the saga of a rich colonial past. The most important monument in Tranquebar is the Dansborg Fort, which is maintained by the local tourist authorities as a museum of Danish and other artefacts. Other important landmarks are the New Jerusalem Church, the Zion Church and some old houses in King's Street. The New Jerusalem Church was built in 1711, with donations from the Danish royal family and its frontage is imprinted with the emblem of the Danish Crown. As a mark of their gratitude, even today, nearly 300 years after its construction, local Christians say prayers every Sunday for the welfare of the Danish royal family. A few years ago, the Danish Government underwrote the cost of repairing the Church.

Tranquebar is also associated with the efforts of the Germans to colonise the Nicobar Islands in the Bay of Bengal and for some time, the Moravian Brethren sent on this colonial mission, stayed in this small Danish town. Some of the old houses in the maritime frontage have what is euphemistically known as 'widow's walks'. These are tall open balconies which were used by the wives from which to watch the seas for the return of their sailor-husbands.

From 1845 to 1860, Tranquebar flourished as the headquarters of Thanjavur district and the District Court and Sessions Court gave added importance to the town. But in 1860, when the railways reached the nearby Nagapatinam port, Tranquebar lost its importance as a town and today languishes as the home of the only Danish castle on Indian shores.

One large mansion built prior to 1845, to house the District Collector, is the sole surviving monument as far as Danish residences are concerned. There were many more Danish-style houses in the early decades of the century, but the last of them was demolished after World War II. Efforts are being made to preserve Tranquebar as a historical link between India and Denmark.

Men who Ruled the Maharajas

It is popularly supposed that the Government of independent India, through their policy of getting the maharajas to 'accede' to India, ended the near-absolute rule of the Indian princes over their domains, covering nearly one third of the Indian subcontinent. But, in reality, the sovereignty over the Indian Princely States was not held by the maharajas, but by the Indian Political Department represented in the State capitals by the British Residents.

In the words of a famous historian, the Department 'sustained as it were, by a continual process of artificial respiration, the princes in their crumpled bastions of antiquated treaties!' Moreover, the Department was the exclusive preserve of the British and very few Indian officers were allowed to 'stray' into it. Among the few notable exceptions was the late K.P.S. Menon, later to become one of the luminaries of independent India's Foreign Ministry.

The Department was solely devoted to the conduct of relations between the British Government and the Indian Princely States (some of them larger than Great Britain), the tribes of the North-West Frontier and with certain potentates beyond the borders of India. Recruitment to it was partly from the ranks of junior civil servants and partly from the officers of the Indian Army — the latter being subject, in the early years of service, to recall to military duty in the event of an emergency.

With the exception of a few top officials stationed at the Secretariat headquarters in Delhi, these officials were scattered all over India in Residencies and Agencies (where a Resident was commonly termed the Political Agent, to a number of small States). Most of the important States like Hyderabad, Kashmir and Gwalior had a Resident of their own and others, like the massed principalities of Rajputana, Kathiawar and Central India, 'shared' a Resident, who was assisted by three or four agents stationed in various parts of these huge areas. It was surprising that the whole number of these appointments, including the headquarters staff for the discharge of responsibilities in relations to 'Indian India' was only about 50 (15 Residents, 13 Political Agents and 4 Political Officers).

The most important duties of the Residents constituted the conduct of relations of the British Government with these States who were prevented by their treaties from having any direct official contact with each other or with any outside power; succession disputes; the training and education of minor rulers; the conduct of the administraiton on behalf of minors and the decision as to whether the ruler was sufficiently mature for powers to be handed over to him. In fact, as Sir Harcourt Butler, one of the luminaries of the Indian Political Department remarked once, 'The life of the average officer of the Indian Political Department was a dog's life with none of the relaxations of the dog'.

There was even an official manual regarding the behaviour of the Resident towards the State ruler and it was a routine duty for every Resident, on assumption of his office, to reiterate formally the sanctity of the mutual treaty pledges to the ruler. The more agreeable aspects were concerned with the pageantry and ceremonies, exchange of official visits and the complicated and magnificent formalities associated with the visits of the Viceroys.

As regards the relationship between the Resident and the ruler, invariably the ruler catered to the whims and fancies of the Resident. In almost all the States, the Resident indirectly wielded so much power, that, even in the early 19th century, His Highness Saktan Thamburan, the greatest ruler the State of Cochin had known, on his death bed advised the heir-apparent, 'not to antagonise the British Resident' and 'never to have anybody as Dewan (chief minister), if he will not promote friendly relations with the British Resident'. His Highness, the Maharaja Swati Thirunal of Travancore State, in the 1830s, found that he had no choice except to commit suicide, if he wished to avoid the British Resident humiliating him. Indeed, as the first States Secretary of independent India, V.P. Menon has explained in his monumental book, *The Integration of Indian States*, 'The progress of each State more or less depended on the character of its Resident'. In the early 1800s, Travancore State had a scholar-General, Cullen, as the Resident and in order to please him, the Maharaja lavished money on education, a worthy cause indeed. At the same time, Mysore had a sportsman — Resident and sports-meets became the fashion of the day. At Indore, the Resident was a lover of horses and the maharaja's stables were full of pedigree horses.

The anxiety of the ruler to please the Resident began to produce, in course of time, an unsatisfactory state of affairs, for the former expended more time in keeping the official in good humour than in analysing the causes of distress among his subjects. The Residents, in turn, since they knew the ruler was chary of getting a bad 'progress Report' from him, became more and more haughty and V.P. Menon relates an incident when one of them ordered a maharaja to wait on him for an interview.

But there were also a number of princes who did not allow the Residents to dictate to them. One such ruler was the late Maharaja of Baroda, Sir Sayaji Rao Gaekwar, who ruled Baroda for more than 60 years and kept the Resident at a 'distance' and this resulted in bitter feelings between him and the Indian Political Department. In the case of Sir Sayaji Rao's predecessor, Maharaja Malhar Rao Gaekwar, the relations had deteriorated to such an extent that in the 1870s, the Government of India felt that there were sufficient grounds for suspecting the Maharaja to have attempted to poison the Resident, Colonel Phayre. Later, a Tribunal consisting of two other maharajas and a Senior British official, absolved the ruler of this accusation, but he was deprived of his throne and exiled to a distant part of India with a handsome allowance.

A Nizam of Hyderabad, the seniormost amongst the Indian rulers, once curtly dismissed the Resident from his presence and the reason for this seems to have been flimsy enough. The year was 1803 and the British Resident at Hyderabad felt that his quarters did not befit the post and that he must have a much larger mansion. Accordingly, he drew the plans on a large sheet of paper and took it to the Nizam for approval. On seeing the 'large paper', the Nizam felt that the Resident's projected mansion might be more magnificent than his own palace and he abruptly dismissed the latter without any comment. The puzzled Resident took the matter to the Nizam's Chief Minister. This official knew of his master's vagaries and understood the real trouble. He advised the Resident to draw the same plan on a smaller piece of paper and then show it to the Nizam, so that the Ruler would not become apprehensive about its size. The Resident followed

British Residency at Hyderabad

this advice and today, the former British Residency at Hyderabad (now a Women's College), is one of the most magnificent buildings in the city. The furniture in its halls was once the property of King George IV and in the 19th century, the expense of keeping the chandeliers burning on festive occasions at Rs 1,000 a night (half a million rupees today), was considered very high for those days.

The relations of the Resident with the other pivotal figure in the State, the Dewan was often more delicate. In many cases, the Dewan, however efficient he might be, had to cater to the whims of both the ruler and the Resident. One eminent Indian administrator, the Dewan of Gwalior, incurred the displeasure of the Resident for having written a letter to him addressed, 'My dear', instead of 'Sir'. But the Dewan stood his ground and the matter was finally sorted out with the Resident having to agree to being addressed in the same manner as he used in his letters to the Dewan. Even Mahatma Gandhi's father, who was the Dewan in a premier Kathiawar State, wilted under the antagonism of the British Resident and had to leave the State. In fact, one of the first occasions the Mahatma was insulted by a British bureaucrat was when a Resident who had known the Mahatma during his London days, had the future liberator of India thrown out of his office.

Even as late as the 1940s, Sir Mirza Ismail, one of the most brilliant administrators of modern India, had to contend with the antagonism of the British Resident in Jaipur State, when he became the Dewan of Jaipur. The British Resident objected to the Dewan 'wasting' money in resusticating the famous gardens of Jaipur.

In spite of the isolation they lived in, very few Residents (except those killed by rebel sepoys during the Sepoy Mutiny of 1857) lost their lives in the discharge of their duties. Two solitary exceptions were those of Manipur State in eastern India and Rampur State in northern India, where, in the 19th century, mobs loyal to the maharajas, killed the Residents for having tried to depose the rulers.

With all their imperialistic bias, many Residents did their duties conscientiously and in the feudal state of affairs that persist in many small Indian States, they were often the sole curbing force. There was a classic instance when the resoluteness of the Resident saved the State capital from being heavily damaged by fire. The temple of the maharaja's family deity caught fire and it spread rapidly to the surrounding buildings. But the orthodox Hindu ruler refused to allow the State Fire Brigade, consisting of non-Hindus, to enter the temple. Rather than have the temple polluted thus, the maharaja preferred to have it burnt down. Unfortunately, the matter would not have ended there and the fire would have spread to other parts of the city. The Resident arrived on the scene at this juncture and spoke sharply to the maharaja. As a result, the Fire Brigade was allowed to enter the temple to extinguish the holocaust.

Residents like General Cullen in Travancore and Colonel Tod in Udaipur (whose book *The Annals of Rajasthan*, is a classic), have left us a rich heritage of records about princely India.

The Residency was legally British territory and in the case

of States like Hyderabad, it formed a small island of British rule in an ocean of surrounding feudalism. Sir Michael O'Dwyer mentions an incident, when he was serving as the British Resident in Hyderabad. Sir O'Dwyer used to receive numerous complaints from the citizens of the surrounding areas that the then Nizam of Hyderabad's English chauffeur, often drove his automobile recklessly in the State and that on many occaisons had seriously injured pedestrians. The police in Hyderabad were most reluctant to take action against the culprit. On one occasion, when the Nizam came to the Residency area, Sir O'Dwyer warned the chauffeur that while it was the Nizam's concern as to how the car was driven in Hyderabad State, in the Residency area it was within British jurisdiciton and that he would not hesitate to hang the driver if he ran over anyone.

The dawn of independence in the Indian subcontinent came as a shock to the Indian Political Department and very few British officials could reconcile themselves to a free India. The last British bureaucrat in charge of the Department, Sir Conrad Corfield, tried his utmost to instigate the Indian princes by telling them that at the stroke of the clock at midnight, on August 14/15, 1947, all of them would become independent sovereigns like the King of Great Britain and that nothing would prevent them from becoming free of the 'yoke' of the independent Republic of India. He advised them to keep out of the Indian Republic. But the newly formed States Ministry of independent India took over from the Political Department and thanks to the innate sense of patriotism displayed by the rulers and the statesmenship of Sardar Patel, the Deputy Prime Minister of India, most of the States, with the exception of Kashmir and Hyderabad, opted for India. Those with a majority of Muslim citizens and contiguous to Pakistan, were to merge with Pakistan. Most British officers preferred to opt for Pakistan or to be pensioned off rather than to continue in service with India. Nostalgic about their connections with the Indian subcontinent, there is still today, an Association of Former Political Officers of the Indian Political Department in UK, although with the march of time, the number of members, most of them in their 80s and 90s, is dwindling.

The Residencies of the numerous Indian States contained many invaluable records about British diplomacy in the East and the interim Indian Government of 1946-47, found to its horror, that the British Residents were systematically burning these records. Five tonnes of valuable records had already been burnt before a joint protest by Jawaharlal Nehru (the first Prime Minister of independent India) and Mohammad Ali Jinnah (the founder of Pakistan), made to the last Viceroy of India, Lord Mountbatten, ensured that, except in the case of documents dealing with the private lives of the maharajas, all other papers would be preserved, subject to the scrutiny of the Imperial Records Commission. The records relating to the private lives of the rulers, were to be taken to Great Britain.

On August 15, 1947, these islands of British rule in 'Indian India' vanished forever, although there were a few stray incidents when the British Residents refused to hoist the Indian tricolor over their erstwhile preserves.

Today, these former Residencies are being used as Government offices in the states and the imposing British Residency in Hyderabad has been converted into a Women's College. But the most famous of all the Residencies is the one that exists only in ruins — the Residency in Lucknow.

Besieged by Indian sepoys during the Sepoy Mutiny, the Residency was reduced to ruins and only the timely arrival of British troops from nearby Cawnpore (Kanpur) saved the British inmates. As a tribute to their heroic stand, the British Union Jack which flew over the ruins of the Residency, was never lowered for 90 years, from 1857 to 1947. The last of these flags was ceremoniously taken down at midnight of August 14 and on his personal command, presented to King George VI, the last Emperor of India, who wanted it for his collection at Windsor Castle.

It was Jawaharlal Nehru's Birthday

It was the year 1889. 'For at least a century to come Indians will not be politically developed enough to be included in the Executive Council' (a body which advised the Viceroy of India on the running of Indian affairs during the days of the Raj). Thus wrote *The Pioneer* of Allahabad, the same week that Jawaharlal Nehru, the first Prime Minister of free India, was born in that town.

A glance at the newspapers of November 14, 1889, the day Jawaharlal Nehru was born, shows that many of today's problems claimed space in the papers then too, like the Irish question and Byculla's sewage problem. Even critics of bureaucracy often take delight in the fact that their cause is a century old! A judge of the Bombay High Court was denied the honour of taking a seat on the Bench on November 14, the first day that the Court met after the vacation all because the written order had not reached him.

Thanks to the newspaper section of the British Library in London, one can peruse the journals of the 19th century, of which complete files are available. Thumbing through the British newspapers — *The Manchester Guardian* (estd. 1821),

The Times (estd. 1785); the Indian metropolitan newspapers such as *The Times of India*, Bombay and *The Englishman*, Calcutta, both already decades-old, as well as *The Pioneer Mail* and *Indian Weekly Mail*, journals of Allahabad, it is possible to gain an overview of the day that marked the birth of India's first Prime Minister.

In Europe, it was the day the Grand Triple Alliance between the Emperors of Germany, Russia and Austria, was to be concluded and the three potentates were due to meet in Innsbruck, Austria, to fix the power equations in Europe. The German Emperor was already in Innsbruck awaiting the Czar of Russia and Emperor Franz Joseph of Austria. His immediate task was to mediate between them to sort out the future of Bulgaria which was being claimed both by Russia and Austria.

In the imperial capital of London, of main interest to India, was the controversial Bill on the increased Indian representation in the Executive Council of the Viceroy and those of the provincial Governors, to be introduced by Charles Bradlaugh, a staunch supporter of the Indian nationalists in Parliament. The British newspapers were sarcastic about his plan to 'involve Indians in the governing of their own country'. Bradlaugh and Sir William Wedderburn, another friend of India, had announced their plans to visit India to confer with the nationalist leaders of the recently formed (four years old) Indian National Congress.

Annie Besant, eventually to become one of India's national leaders, was fighting a Court case on the day, in defence of her educational principles. A new Lord Mayor of London had been elected. Hence, his inauguration, together with the 48th birthday celebrations of the Prince of Wales, gave a gala atmosphere to the Empire's First City.

Among more mundane events was a meeting planned in Leeds to protest against the opium traffic in India and China.

The Irish terrorists were as active as now and the Parnell Commission appointed by the British Government was in session on November 14, 1889, to investigate the Irish Republican Brotherhood, one of the Irish nationalist groups.

In India, the most noteworthy news item was the State visit of H.R.H. Prince Albert Victor, the third son of Queen Victoria. He had come to India earlier in the year and on November 14, was at Poona, being fêted by the Governor of Bombay Lord Reay and other satraps. The Maharajas of Kolhapur and Miraj were in Poona to welcome the Prince.

The Viceroy himself, was touring the North Western Frontier Province and was at Dera Ismail Khan, holding a durbar of tribal chiefs. The weather over the subcontinent was good and *The Times of India* reported that the cotton crop was expected to be excellent. Among other economic indicators, the price of silver rose to 44 pence per ounce from 42 pence (from Rs 63 rupees a kg to Rs 66).

On November 14, 1889, in Kabul Afghanistan, a caravanserai frequented by Indian traders, was destroyed by fire and the loss was estimated by some at Rs 5 lakhs. 'It was probably over estimated', wrote *The Times of India.*

The sewage system of Bombay city was in as bad a state as now, and on November 14, the Byculla Club, at its special meeting, had condemned the apathy of the civic officials. The luxury yacht of the Gaekwar of Baroda, *S.S. Zingara*, had run aground on rocks near Alibagh, Bombay and the Bombay dockyard authorities were trying their best to save the ship from getting wrecked.

In Calcutta, then the capital of India, the Municipal Corporation was debating the need to appoint a Health officer and the Indian Army Headquarters were sending reinforcement for the Chin-Lushai expedition.

In the northern districts of the United Provinces (modern Uttar Pradesh), an improved version of the Bareilly dandi or sedan chair-like facility to carry tourists up the mountain slopes, had been devised with a mechanism 'which will always keep the dandi on an even keel, whether taken up or down the hills. Its greatest advantage was that the memsahibs using the dandi would not feel embarassed by the oscillations of the dandi, revealing their knickers', wrote *The Pioneer* of Allahabad. Indeed, European dignity had been maintained.

In Allahabad, Nehru's hometown, the most important news journals were the anglophile *The Pioneer Mail* and *Indian Weekly Mail*. Every week, special edition of the journal printed on Wednesday night, was the masthead proudly proclaimed, 'Published on the night of despatch for Europe of the Overland Mail via Bombay and Brindisi' and the issue dated November 20, 1889, which covered the period from November 14 to November 20, 1889, listed province by province, the important events of the week.

The journal discussed Charles Bradlaugh's Bill to be introduced in the House of Commons named the 'Draft Bill for reforming the Supreme and Legislative Councils'. The *Pioneer* felt that this Bill, was premature. It asserted that 'India, for at least a century to come would not be politically developed enough to merit such representation'.

Allen Octavian Hume, the founder of the Indian National Congress, four years earlier, was to visit Bombay and different welcome demonstrations planned by the Indians made the *Pioneer* cynical, as to how such a group of disparate people were going to forge a nation, capable of governing themselves.

A rise in transport charges was engaging the attention of the Englishmen resident in India. The near monopoly of the P&O Line (the Peninsular and Orient Line) on the Bombay-London route, was held to be responsible for this and a national association known as the Anglo-Indian Cheap Passage Association, met in Allahabad on November 14. It demanded that the charges be kept at Rs 700 for a double ticket for London-Bombay and Rs 560 for a London-Bombay return ticket. It we consider the purchasing power of the 1889 Indian rupee, the present day fares are very economical.

Of ironical note is the fact that the infant Jawaharlal, a future Prime minister of India and despite being the son of one of the most outstanding lawyers of Allahabad, could not even make it to the births columns of the *Pioneer*. The *Pioneer* issue covering the week ending November 20, 1889, contained one Indian name amongst the eight 'arrivals', the other seven being English babies. The lone Indian child was one Jadu Nath Bose, son of the subdivisional officer of the district of Katwa, born on November 2, 1889. Nehru's handicap was that he was not the son of any Government official. Well, the Indian newspapers of November 14/15, 1889, thus gave no hint of the birth of one of the titans of modern India, in fact, its first Prime Minister.

The Great White Mutiny

Although the Sepoy Mutiny was quelled within two years of its eruption, its aftereffects lingered. In the decades following the insurrection, the disparity between the white and brown communities became even more marked.

Queen Victoria had given the assurance in her Proclamation of 1858, that, 'There is no hatred to the brown skin, none whatsoever'. But as far as the British resident in India was concerned, they were citizen subjects and the Indians subject citizens. The brunt of this antagonism was directed against the rising generation of educated Indians, the alumni of the newly established Universities of Bombay, Calcutta and Madras. Unlike the peasant in rural areas and the merchant in the cities, these 'hybridised Indians with their English Education and ideals, often showed a rather undesirable tendency' to political aspirations.

But the British Government in London, 6000 miles away from the scene, never really understood the chasm that divided the British in India and the English educated Indians. As such, their reforms and redresses, well-meant but often formulated without taking into consideration this ever-widening gulf in the Indian political scene, came to nought.

The very first step that shocked the British resident in

India, was the success of one Indian, Satyendra Nath Tagore, in the ICS (Indian Civil Service) examination of 1864. As early as 1853, the system of nomination to the Covenanted Services had been replaced by one of competition among all natural born subjects of Her Majesty and even then, there had been widespread resentment at the 'opening of the heaven born services' to Indians. Further, the Government of India, by the Act of 1870, made it clear that one-fifth of all new recruits to the ICS should be Indian and the Indian 'infiltration' became regular in the 1870s.

Lord Ripon

Thus, when Lord Ripon (later to be known to Indians as Ripon the Righteous) became the Viceroy of India in 1880, the British resident in India was in a sullen mood. Many 'influential quarters' suggested to Ripon that Indians should be barred from the ICS and that those already employed should be got rid of by paying them compensation. But the Viceroy, with his liberal attitude to the Indian masses, refused to oblige. Further, as the years went by, he had a very difficult task to ensure that in their motherland India, Indians obtained a fair share of the posts in the higher cadres of the administration. As all these posts were then held by Englishmen, purportedly to be handed over from British to British, the Viceroy soon became the target of British imperialists in India. The climax came in 1882, when the Chief Justice of the Calcutta High Court, Sir Richard Garth, took two months leave. According to the conventions, the next senior judge was to officiate as the Chief Justice during the leave period and Ripon found that Justice Romesh Chandra Mitter was to be appointed as the Acting Chief Justice.

The Viceroy did not have to take the advice of the Lieutenant-Governor of Bengal, but still he sounded him for his views. The Lieutenant-Governor realised that he had no choice but to recommend Mitter for the post. But at the same time, if it was widely known that the Governor had acquiesced with the Viceroy, the European community in Calcutta would feel let down by him. He therefore advised the Viceroy that while Mitter was a good Civil Judge he had no experience of criminal trials and recommended Justice Cunningham, the next in seniority to Mitter, for the post.

When the Chief Justice, Sir Richard Garth, heard rumours that the Viceroy proposed to appoint Mitter for the post, he was 'shocked' and wrote to the Viceroy that rather than see an Indian occupy the august post, he would give up the leave. But Ripon refused to be intimidated and in 1882, for the first time in its history, the Calcutta High Court had an Indian Chief Justice officiating for two months.

Thus, by 1882, Lord Ripon had become the pet aversion of all Anglophiles in India. It was at this juncture that the consideration of a sober memorandum sent to Sir Ashley Eden, the Lieutenant-Governor of Bengal, by Beharilal Gupta, an Indian Covenanted Civil Servant, regarding the

Code of Criminal Procedure, touched off the explosion known as the Great White Mutiny to contemporary historians.

Although not as well known and less violent than the Great Sepoy Mutiny, the after-effects of the Great White Mutiny was more disastrous to the British. Whereas the Sepoy Mutiny wiped the slate clean for British supremacy in India, the White Mutiny, by its very nature, cleft in two the hope of the British Government to stabilise the 'rule of a small minority of one race over a vast population of another'.

The reason for this turbulence in Indian politics was complicated enough. Before 1857, in the Indian territories under the East India Company, there were two separate systems of Law and Jurisdiction. The first was the Muhammaden Law administered in the rural areas by the Company's Court, based upon the *de jure* authority of the Mughal Emperor. The second was British Law, administered in the Presidency towns of Bombay, Madras and Calcutta by the High Courts. Lord Dalhousie and his predecessors had felt that it would be unfair to submit the British in India to Muhammaden Law and as such, except in the Presidency towns, where Justice was administered as per British Law, no Indian Judge could try criminal cases against European/British subjects. But they were allowed to try all civil cases involving Europeans. Then, the Indian Penal Code of 1861, gave the country a uniform Criminal Law and in the same year High Courts were established, supreme over all courts in the Presidency towns and the mofussil courts.

This reform should have, in all fairness, removed the disparity in the power wielded by an Indian member of the Judicial Services and should have ensured that an Indian magistrate in the mofussil would be able to try criminal cases against European subjects, just as he was authorised to do in the Presidency towns. But this lacuna in the law was not removed. In the initial stages, as long as the number of British in mofussil districts were few, this anomaly did not interfere with the course of justice. But in later years, as the number of non-official British, like the indigo planters, the coal mine managers, the railway officials, increased in the interior districts, justice was often delayed and denied to the victims in criminal cases, involving European British subjects.

The memorandum Behari Lal Gupta, a Presidency Magistrate of Calcutta, submitted to Sir Ashley Eden, sought to remove this anomaly and Gupta pointed out that while officiating as Presidency Magistrate, he had exercised powers which he had to forfeit on receiving a more responsible appointment in the mofussil.

Sir Ashley Eden realised the invidious position the Indian members were placed in by this distinction between mofussil and Presidency magistrates and his views advocating the removal of this aniomaly were circulated to provincial Governments for their opinion. The civilian members of the Viceroy's Executive Council opposed the reforms, but the Governors of Bengal, Bombay, Madras, NWFP, the Commander-in-Chief of the Indian Army, the Chief Commissioners of the Central Provinces, British Burma, Assam and the Resident at Hyderabad, all favoured the grant of jurisdiction while the Chief Commissioner of Coorg opposed the measure for 'political' reasons. But as events proved, none of these high officials gauged the possible reactions of non-official British regarding the matter.

As such, the Viceroy, guided by the opinions of the Governors, proceeded with his intentions, deeming the matter to be nothing more than rectifying a minor lacuna in law. In October 1882, the views of the Viceroy and his Executive Council were sent to the Secretary of State for India and his Council in London. The Legal Adviser to the Secretary of State, Maine, was away in Paris and the Viceroy's despatch was sent to him for his remarks. Maine, while agreeing with the reasonableness of the steps to be taken, felt that the British resident in India would react violently against the measures and suggested that the Viceroy should elicit the opinion of British non-officials in India, before proceeding with the Bill.

This warning was supposed to be conveyed to the Viceroy privately by Hartington, another member of the Council of the Secretary of State. But Hartington kept Maine's letter in his pocket and completely forgot about it. The aftereffect of this lapse of memory was to shake the very foundations and the stability of the Indian Empire.

The Viceroy, when he received the communication from the Secretary of State, found no advice to elicit the opinion of the British resident in India and therefore asked Sir Courtney Ilbert, the Law Member of his Executive Council, to proceed with the Bill. On February 2, 1883, Sir Ilbert introduced the Bill (thus known as the Ilbert Bill), embodying the extension of the jurisdiction of the Indian magistrates.

Since the Act of 1861 had stated that only a Justice of Peace (JP) could exercise jurisdiction over British residents in India in criminal cases, the Bill was mainly directed towards making Indians eligible to become JPs. The main points were that, irrespective of their race, Covenanted Civil Servants, members of the Civil Services constituted under the Statutory Rules, Assistant Commissioners in non-regulation provinces and cantonment magistrates, being magistrates of the first class, were eligible to become JPs and were thus empowered to try British persons in criminal cases. Sessions Judges and District Magistrates were to be ex-officio JPs. An Assistant Sessions Judge was not to exercise jurisdiction over a European/British subject, unless he had held the office for three years and after he had been empowered to do so by the local Governments. But so few were the Indians in the higher cadres of the Government of India, that not more than 37

Indians all over India would have qualified for judging criminal cases in which Europeans were involved.

But, when on February 2, 1883, the Bill was published, the British residents in India were aghast at the 'equal status given to Indians'. Jawaharlal Nehru, quotes in his book, *Discovery of India*, that Seton Carr, who was the Foreign Secretary to the Government of India at that time, declared that this Bill outraged the cherished conviction which was shared by every British resident in India, from the highest to the lowest, by the plantation assistant in his lowly bungalow and by the editor in the full light of the Presidency towns to the Viceroy on his throne, that he belonged to a race, whom God had destined to govern and subdue Indians.

A huge meeting was held in the Town Hall of Calcutta by the British, attended by nearly 3000 members and speeches of an extremely intemperate and indecent nature were made against the Government of India. 'This Bill has been brought at the instance of a few greasy bloated *baboos*', shouted Mr. Branson, a leading member of the British community and swore that come what may, he would never allow a 'nigger' to sit in judgement over him. There was even a proposal to march to the nearby Government House, to protest against the Bill. But later, it was decided to postpone the demonstration. Though the storm centred in Calcutta, European Clubs and Associations all over India took up the cry and the demonstrations were mainly subsidised and supported by those who had a great stake in the mofussil areas, namely the indigo planters and the tea planters. Thousands of Indian labourers worked in the plantations and often cases were brought against the plantation managers, usually Europeans, for having assaulted the labourers. As long as a British person sat in judgement over them, the managers hoped to escape with light punishment. But now, if the Ilbert Bill was to become law, they would have to submit themselves to Indian

Judges, who may not have viewed with sympathy the rights of the ruling races.

As the official in charge of the Criminal investigation Department (CID) reported to the Viceroy's Private Secretary, 'To make their grievance a general one, the British raised the cry of danger to European women'. Indian judges, the agitators claimed, would abuse the jurisdiction to fill their harems with white women.

'Would you like to live in a country?' queried the editor of *Friend of India*, in his Anglophile journal of Calcutta, 'where at any moment your wife would be liable to be sentenced on a false charge of slapping the *ayah*, the magistrate being a copper-coloured pagan, who probably worships the *linga* and certainly exults in any opportunity of showing that he can insult white persons with impunity!' In fact, with the honoured exception of *The Statesman* of Calcutta, the European journals in India began a concerted attack on the Bill.

As the crescendo mounted, the Viceroy realised that he had unwittingly created a very dangerous situation. Scarcely 25 years had elapsed since the Sepoy Mutiny was quelled and now, unlike then, there was an Indian press to reply in kind. Already the first reactions to the European's vituperations had come from the *Amrita Bazar Patrika*, which wrote on March 1, 1883, 'The dominant race may object to be tried by a nigger, but the European forger can have no reason to object to be put on equal terms with a native forger'. In the important cities of India, like Bombay, Madras and Calcutta, sober Indian statesman like the 'Grand Old Man of India', Dadabhai Naoroji and Sir Phirozshah Mehta, were declaiming to huge audiences supporting the Bill and in Calcutta, Indian advocates were withdrawing their cases from British barristers supporting the agitation agaisnt the Bill. Further, Indian public opinion was planning huge demonstrations to support the Viceroy against the European agitators.

In fact, the feeling between the educated section of Indians and the British in India, ran so high that *Punch*, of London, printed a cartoon showing an elephant (India) with Ripon as its mahout and a number of Europeans leaning out of the howdah to attack him, the caption reading, 'Anglo-Indian Mutiny ... a bad example to the elephant'. The Viceroy knew that this was no exaggerated picture.

In Calcutta, a European and Anglo-Indian Defence Association was formed to protect British women in India from Indian Judges and Lady Garth, wife of the Chief Justice, Sir Richard Garth, collected the signatures of hundreds of European and Anglo-Indian women to petition against the Bill.

But it would have been a great defeat for the Government of India were it to withdraw the reforms, even though it was only a Bill and the Viceroy tried his best to reason with his opponents. For over forty years, Indian magistrates had tried civil cases concerning British citizens and there had been no complaints, he pointed out and declared that as far as the reforms were concerned, he was determined to carry them out and would not heed 'to violence, to exaggeration, to misrepresentation and least of all to menace'.

But his compatriots in India were in no mood to listen. Their leaders warned the British in India about the 'wily natives, who creep in where you cannot walk, unless you walk upright'. The most violent amongst them did not hesitate to prophesy civil war in India, and British volunteers in the Indian Army were urged to resign en masse. Further, in the canteens of British soldiers, opinions were sounded as to their reaction if the bill was passed. The English tea planters in Assam promised to lynch any Indian judge who would have the temerity to sit in judgement over a criminal case involving European/British subjects.

Attempts were made to stir up public opinion in England

by painting lurid pictures of the nighmarish existence facing the British resident in lonely districts. One Atkins was equipped with funds and sent to England to stir the working classes there against the Bill. Atkins, however, failed to win the British public to his side and as Lord Northbrook wrote to Ripon, 'At Atkins's most important meeting in Edinburgh, a motion was carried unanimously against him.'

But in Calcutta, the seat of the Government of India in those days, the tempo of the agitation increased and the climax came when Lord Ripon arrived from Simla on December 1, to spend Christmas in Calcutta. The European and Anglo-Indian Defence Association had imported scores of British planters from the mofussil and the whole mob congregated close to Government House. As the Viceroy's carriage drew near the mob, he started to bow to them but quickly realised their mood and carried on without making the customary bow. As if by signal, the whole mob began to hoot and jeer the Viceroy, an unprecedented event, even in the days of the Sepoy Mutiny. Further, at the annual Viceregal Levee, all non-official Europeans stayed away from the function and whenever the Viceroy ventured into the streets, he was insulted by Europeans who assumed a theatrical air of insolence towards him. At the annual parade of the Indian Army, scarcely 20 of the British Volunteers turned up and during a banquet held on St. Andrew's Day, a stony silence greeted the guest toasting the Viceroy's health.

But the Viceroy, fortified by the behaviour of the educated class of Indians, who behaved with great moderation and forebearance, refused to turn back and the European and Anglo-Indian Defence Association decided on more violent measures. The first step proposed was to invite the maximum possible number of European residents to Calcutta from the mofussil for a huge demonstration, if the Bill should become law.

The second was a conspiracy to overpower the sentries at Government House in Calcutta, arrest the Viceroy, put him aboard a steamer at Chandpal Ghat in Calcutta and deport him to England via the Cape of Good Hope. It does seem rather unbelievable that the British residents of India should have decided on such an extreme step. But Sir Henry Cotton remarks in his book, *India and Home Memories*, that the Lieutenant Governor of Bengal, Sir Rivers Thompson and the Commissioner of Police, Calcutta, knew of the conspiracy. Sir Rivers Thompson himself was one of the 'invisible' hands behind the agitation and he did not even warn the Viceroy about the conspiracy. The tea planters of Assam, 'of whom much was expected', had their own plan to kidnap the Viceroy. Months earlier they had assembled at Darjeeling to jeer and hoot the Viceroy as his special train passed by and it was with difficulty that the Viceroy prevented his *aide-de-camp* from jumping on the platform to chastise the mob. Lord Ripon was scheduled to go on a shikar in Assam and plans were made by the planters to kidnap him. But somehow the Viceroy's entourage got news of this conspiracy and Lord Ripon's son went on the shikar instead of his father.

The Viceroy was not at all worried about the kidnapping scares. But he was very apprehensive about the huge meeting that was to be assembled in Calcutta. In 1883, the total number of British in India (including 55,760 soldiers) was 89,793 — a microcosm among the millions of Indians. In Calcutta, there were nearly 7000 British. If the European planters ended the 'monster' meeting in a racial riot between Indians and Europeans, what was he to do? The whole strength of the European police in Calcutta was no more than 70 and calling out British troops to suppress the white 'Mutineers' would have created an explosive situation.

In England, the Home Government had firmly given their support to the Viceroy's decision to proceed with the Bill. But in India, only one member of his Executive Council, Ilbert, had supported the Bill in its final form and he was urged by the other Members of the Council to make concessions in the Bill. Evans, the leader of the European agitators, had promised to wind up the Defence Association if the Viceroy would relent. Finally, Lord Ripon asked the Finance Member of his Executive Council, Colvin, to discuss the bill with Evans and gave him full powers to arrive at a compromise. And on January 25, 1884, a Bill based on the Colvin-Evans Concordat was enacted. According to this Concordat, the original proposals were withdrawn and instead, new provisions were substituted which passed into law. European British subjects were to have the right to claim trial by a Jury of 12, at least 7 of whom must be European/British subjects. If in the mofussil districts no jury could be formed, the magistrate could have the case transferred to such other court as the High Court might direct.

The British community in India was jubilant at the victory, although in principle, Indian judges had equal rights with those of their European colleagues. As for the Indians, especially those of the educated classes, whose competence to sit in judgement over European/British subjects was the point of dispute, the overwhelming feeling was that the compromise, especially that of having a jury with a majority of British in it, was worse than having the Bill withdrawn. Although the battle was won, the citadel was lost.

In the words of Sir Ashley Eden, a former Lieutenant Governor of Bengal, the Ilbert Bill excited a fiercer and more perilous conflict of races than was witnessed in the Mutiny and it was nearly forty years later, in 1923, that a Bill called the Racial Distinction Bill, was passed into law, with scarcely a dissident voice and removed the important differences in the trial of British citizens and Indians.

But unwittingly, the British residents in India had

instructed Indians in constitutional agitation. The leaders of Indian nationalism had watched from the sidelines this grand struggle between the Viceroy and the British populace in India, the former in his own right the most powerful official in the world and further supported by the Home Government in Britain. But, to their surprise, the Indian leaders found that, confronted by this agitation engineered by the British in India, the Viceroy had no choice but to retreat.

As such, it was no coincidence that the first meeting of the Indian National Congress, an organisation that was to spearhead the nationalist struggle for freedom, was held two years later in 1885.

An Indian Patriot in British Parliament

The struggle for freedom from the British yoke was waged by Indians in different ways, ranging from Mahatma Gandhi's non-violent methods to Subhas Chandra Bose's formation of the Indian National Army, with the help of the Japanese. But very few thought of carrying the fight to the British Parliament and it was Dadabhai Naoroji, the second President of the Indian National Congress, who decided to get himself elected to the British Parliament and so carry on the struggle in the highest forum of the British Empire.

Now, a century later, it is difficult to appreciate the uphill task that faced the 'Grand Old Man of India' in his attempt to win a seat for India in the British Parliament of 1891. Scarcely three decades had passed since the Sepoy Mutiny and to the average British citizen, an Indian connoted nothing more than idolatrous pagans. It is not known exactly when Dadabhai Naoroji was inspired with the resolve to stand for election in England. For 30 years since 1855, he had been resident in England and he had built up a name for integrity and honesty. Even the conservative Bank of England had great respect for this Indian businessman, especially as he had met

Dadabhai Naoroji

all his financial commitments in full in 1866, when at the end of the American Civil War, the cotton market in India collapsed and many Indian businessmen became insolvent.

Having presided over the second session of the Indian National Congress in 1886, he seems to have thought of entering British Parliament and doing his best there to propagate India's views on Home Rule and other reforms. But at the same time, he was fully aware of the stupendous nature of the task and wanted to proceed with discretion, so that if it was found to be impossible, he could abandon the project without any loss of face. He consulted some of his colleagues in the Indian National Congress and while many of them were enthusiastic, the general attitude was that even if he succeeded, nothing concrete could be done in Parliament. 'What can you do alone single handed in that vast assembly and we want you here in India', was the general tenor of their opinions.

Eminent British friends of India such as Sir William Wedderburn and Lord Ripon, were sceptical about the plan, while his political foe and personal friend, Sir George Birdwood, felt that even for an Englishman, it was difficult to win a seat in the general elections. Despite these discouragements, Dadabhai Naoroji decided to take a chance and returned to London with letters of introduction to eminent Party leaders. But here too, his ambition was greeted with polite surprise. The doyen of Liberal Party leaders, John Bright, advised Dadabhai Naoroji that, 'A man had to be either a local notable or one of great distinction' and another British statesman confided to him that, 'In any case the candidature is decided mainly on party affiliations and never on merits'.

But it was not the first time that an Indian was standing for election to the British Parliament. In the last two general elections prior to 1891, the Liberal party had nominated Lal Mohan Ghose for a seat from Deptford and he had lost on both occasions. Thus, some Liberal Party leaders advised Naoroji to stand from a Scottish or Irish constituency, where the conservatives were not so strong and pro-Imperialist passions might not be so persistent. British friends vainly requested Naoroji to discard his Parsi headgear for an English hat, so that his Indian origin might not be so conspicuous. Lal Mohan Ghose, with his own experiences in mind, advised him that he would require extensive funds to contest the elections and remarked that lack of money had been instrumental in his own defeats.

Finally, after much spadework, the Liberal Party invited Naoroji to stand from the St. Alban's constituency in London. But Dadabhai Naoroji found on scrutiny of the voting records of the past, that the Conservative Party was so strong in that area that there was absolutely no chance for him in that constituency and so declined the offer. Finally, nine days before the voters were to elect a new Parliament, the Liberal Party agreed to support him from the Holborn constituency and 'Dadabhai Naoroji, an eminent native of India', was introduced to the voter as the Liberal Party candidate.

Speaking about those hectic nine days, the Indian candidate remarked later that it was really a nine day wonder, at the end of which, he lost the elections. But he did not spare any effort to put himself, an utter stranger in the constituency, in the public eye and was in fact doing the spadework for the next elections rather than working with hopes of success in the current ones. Because he was a candidate from Holborn, the newspapers spread the news of an Indian standing against the 'native' Englishman in his own constituency, far and wide. When the final results were announced, Naoroji received 1950 votes against 3651 received by his conservative opponent, Colonel Duncan. The Indian leader wrote to Lord Ripon later, that he would have won but for the split among the Liberal Party members. Of those who were entitled to vote in the elections, there were a total of 3000 non-voters. But Naoroji had fought a clean battle and at the end of the elections, his rival publicly thanked him for his courtesy during the campaign.

The next elections were at least six years away and Naoroji, with all his zeal, nevertheless found it difficult to keep up his political campaigns in full gear. If he had devoted himself to business, finances would have been no problem. But as a politician, he had very meagre resources. In fact, his private means enabled him to stay in London for just two years and that too without his incurring any expenses to 'cultivate' his political electors. Initially there was a proposal from his Indian friends to collect sufficient funds to enable him to carry on his work, but eventually this did not materialize.

Naoroji somehow carried on in London and within barely two years of his failure, a chance to be nominated as the Liberal candidate from the Central Finsbury constituency came his way. In March 1888, Honourable Howard Spensley, the Liberal candidate, who was being groomed for the general elections from Finsbury, resigned, throwing open the door for Liberal Party members to compete for the nomination. Finally, after eight ballots spread over six months, Dadabhai Naoroji's name led the list. But one technical hitch developed over the final balloting, after the results had been announced officially, as some of Naoroji's opponents felt that some points of procedure had been overlooked. Attempts were made by them to persuade the Indian leader to agree to arbitration over the final nomination. But Naoroji knew that he had won the nomination in a fair manner and that the attempts now being made, were just to deprive him of his chance and so refused to accept the arbitration proposal. This caused a split in the Liberal Party ranks and till a few days prior to polling Naoroji was opposed by the Conservative party candidate, as well as by an independent Liberal, who had official backing. But a last minute intervention by Lord Ripon caused by the party to unite behind the Indian candidate and the election was a straight contest between the Indian leader and his Conservative rival, Captain Penton.

But even with this reconciliation, Dadabhai Naoroji's attempt might not have succeeded but for a major blunder by the Conservative Party leader and the British Prime minister, Lord Salisbury. During one of his campaign speeches, on November 30, 1891, Lord Salisbury slightingly referred to Naoroji as a 'Black Man' and expressed the hope that true Englishmen would not elect a 'Black Man' to represent them in Parliament.

Used as the British public was to election misrepresentations and character smears, this attack on a rival's race and colour was shocking and Dadabhai Naoroji was flooded with letters from British citizens, expressing indignation at Lord Salisbury's statement. Eminent statesmen like Gladstone and Morley, wanted the Prime Minister to apologise to Naoroji and it was known that Queen Victoria was very much displeased by this undignified statement made by her own Prime Minister, aimed against one of her Indian subjects. It was rumoured that the Queen had pointed out to him that she had millions of Indian subjects, who would not relish such a remark made by her own Prime Minister.

In any case, Dadabhai Naoroji overnight became the most celebrated Indian in England. Associations, clubs and societies, till then lukewarm in their support to him, enthusiastically rallied to his side. Naoroji could have rebutted Lord Salisbury's remark by pointing out that a year earlier, the Prime Minister had invited this 'Black Man' to become a member of the Governing Board of the Imperial Institute. But rather he chose the course of dignified silence.

The Conservative journals in Finsbury, however, did not observe any such decorum and tried their utmost to prejudice the electors against Naoroji. One journal represented him as a fire-worshipping pagan and asked God-fearing Christians not to vote for him. In fact, of all the stigmas his opponents foisted on him, the one Naoroji found most difficult to explain to the average English voter, was that of being a fire-worshipping pagan and quite a number of orthodox Christians were misled by this fanatical remark.

St. Stephen's Review, a local journal, felt that the only nice thing about Naoroji's candidature was that it was better than having a Bengali Baboo as a candidate (an indirect hint at Lal Mohan Ghose). It derisively told its readers, 'Central Finsbury should be ashamed of itself, having publicly confessed that there was not in the whole of the Division, an Englishman, a Scotsman, Welshman or an Irishman, as worthy of their votes as this fire-worshipper from Bombay.'

A retired Indian Army officer, writing in the *Morning Post*, gratuitously informed readers that, 'Dadabhai Naoroji is an alien in India, belonging to a race of mere traders, none of whom ever drew a sword, or pulled a trigger either for or against us, a people who, if we were to leave India, would be massacred to a man by the fighting races'.

As election day drew nearer, the Indian candidate found to his dismay, that his Conservative opponent being a rich man, had cornered all the coaches for transporting his supporters to the polls and besides this, aristocratic gentry like Lord Salisbury, had loaned him their carriages for the task. As it was, Naoroji was running short of money for his election expenses and to arrange for carriages at such short notice, was a difficult task. Happily for him, Sir Sayaji Rao Gaekwar, the Maharaja of Baroda, who was keenly following the contest, countered the rival's move by arranging hired carriages for transporting Naoroji's voters to the polls and this saved the day for the Indian leader. Finally, when the election results were declared, Dadabhai Naoroji had won by three votes. He had secured 2959 votes against 2956 for Captain Penton who demanded a recount. Quite a number of legal petitions were made by him before he conceded defeat six months later. The average English voter, who did not know how to pronounce Dadabhai Naoroji's name, was offered an epithet by the newspapers — 'Naoroji or Narrow majority'. He retained this seat for four years, till he was defeated in the general elections of 1895, by a majority of 800 votes.

During the years he was in Parliament, he was in a place where the powers of the Government of India could not touch him and the British Parliament was informed about the problems of India by one of her own sons. Now, more than a hundred years later, one can look back with pride at the achievement of the 'Grand Old Man of India', who bearded the Imperialist British Lion, in its own den.

Mahatma Gandhi — Historians Delve into the Mystery of his Leadership

Some time ago, one of the close associates of Mahatma Gandhi was reminiscensing about the secret behind the Mahatma's leadership. One was surprised to hear him say poignantly, 'In those days, when the communications systems were not so efficient, the Mahatma had hundreds of co-workers spread over the whole Indian subcontinent, as well as in different countries. He kept a watch over all their activities and knew how they would react to any situation in the interest of humanity. He even persuaded Sardar Patel, a great pragmatist, who had been chosen by the Congress Party to be the first Prime Minister of India, to withdraw in favour of the utopian idealist Nehru. But today, in the electronic age, our so-called leaders, who claim to be his followers, are not able to guide the nation nor to keep track of what is happening in the next room!'

What was indeed the mystique of the leadership of the Mahatma, whose disciples ranged from the aristocratic Nehru to the ascetic Vinobha Bhave?

Dr. Rajendra Prasad, the first President of India, who was one of the favourite disciples of the Mahatma, once suggested to him that he should write a book explaining his principles of leadership, somewhat like a text book, so that his followers could refer it for guidance. The Mahatma replied, 'This is not my business nor can I do so, for I am always experimenting with Truth and testing all new ideas as they come to me on the touchstone of Truth. In this process there is always the possibility of errors. These errors may require correction the very next day. Tell me, how can I write such a book?'

Further, according to Dr. Rajendra Prasad, 'We were not able to get a comprehensive view of his ideas and each of us engaged himself in some activity according to the Mahatma's teachings.'

Over the decades, quite a number of theses have been written on the Mahatma's qualities of leadership. Professor Wolfenstein, comparing the personalities of Lenin, Trotsky and Gandhi, picked out the following qualities as contributory to leadership — trust, pride, courage, industry, confidence and drive. Comparing Gandhi and Lenin, Wolfenstein found that the Indian saint-statesman was a better leader when action without premeditation was required.

For the Mahatma, courage meant the ability to suffer pain and face death rather than the commonplace connotation of being able to inflict and guard against death. His main method in dealing with any situation, was to turn an aggressive confrontation into a peaceful enterprise. Whereas Lenin viewed himself as aloof in a hostile world, the Mahatma considered his surroundings as capable of great harmony and truth.

The Mahatma's approach to life made it possible for him to bring out a spontaneous responsiveness from his followers, which quality Lenin lacked.

The Mahatma and Lenin in particular, believed that lack of emotional control, whatever be the nature of the emotion, was dangerous. But Lenin, who was basically mistrustful and who had a firmer identification with the masculine figures in his life, felt that love was more dangerous than hate, passivity more of a risk than activity. The Mahatma, who was more trustful and feminine, reversed the faith formula and felt hatred and aggression were more likely to lead to unhappy consequences than love.

Again, compared to Lenin, at whose death, the war of succession divided the party, the Indian leader ensured that there would be a smooth transition. This was because he did not relish bearing office himself. Thus, not a murmur came from the party ranks when he chose Nehru to lead the nation.

Mahatma Gandhi

The famous writer, Pearl S. Buck, comparing Mahatma Gandhi and Dr. Sun Yat Sen, the Father of modern China, opined that a capacity for dreaming is necessary in any leader. Dr. Sun Yat Sen was a dreamer, he had the qualities of a genius but no talent to make dreams come true. But Mahatma Gandhi, while having the same genius as the Chinese leader, had a remarkable talent for practical application. The way he dramatized events was shown by his resolve, when after seeing ill-clad farmers in Orissa, he chose their dress as his uniform and thus endeared himself to the Indian masses to the last. His dramatization of the Salt Satyagraha was the acme of showmanship, when by symbolically picking a few crystals of salt from a deserted sea shore, he helped topple an Empire.

Another aspect of the Mahatma was that he identified himself with the humblest and in India this sincere gesture of humility served as the basis for actual leadership.

Perhaps the most important facet of the Mahatma's leadership was the gift of selecting the right man for carrying out his multifarious activities. He assigned work according to intelligence, education, way of life and abilities. One aspect of his uncanny knack of finding the correct man for the correct job, showed itself in his attitude towards non-violence. Dr. Rajendra Prasad says, 'While his confidence in non-violence was unshakeable, he wanted to enlist the co-operation of those, who were not prepared to go so far in observing non-violence.'

Another quality which struck many of his followers was his fortitude, even in times of deep sorrow. Although he confessed in speeches that he had no more wish to live, yet he worked on undaunted, showing the same courtesy, gentleness, firmness and sweetness to his endless visitors, helping all who came to him, day by day, to find things, even when the world around was grim and overpowering.

A factor that moved his followers was the intense personal concern he showed to them even when he differed from them and chastised them. Even the humblest of his co-workers knew that besides their work as his colleagues in the freedom struggle, the Mahatma was personally interested in their welfare.

Dr. Sudhir Ghosh, who carried out many important assignments as his emissary, states that once the Mahatma sent him to London for a long stay to carry on confidential discussions with the British Cabinet. Before he left for London, the Mahatma told him that in case Ghosh took his physician-wife with him, she should join a medical institute to further her knowledge. A few months later, the political situation in India took a turn for the worse and the Mahatma asked Ghosh to return. Ghosh was puzzled as to what he should do regarding his wife, who had enrolled herself at a medical college for advance studies. But his problem was solved the next day, when a telegram came from the Mahatma asking forgiveness for not referring to Mrs. Ghosh. He felt that she should stay back in London and finish the course. This kind of fatherliness in the saint-statesman, even when involved in intricate national political problems, made his followers absolutely loyal to him.

Even stray guests to the Ashram felt this warm and humane concern of the great leader. Once an American missionary brought to the Mahatma at Wardha, a message from a political leader. The Mahatma was sitting under a tree and as the misionary advanced towards him, a low hanging branch hit his forehead. The Mahatma immediately asked the Ashram physician to give him first aid. Years later, when the same missionary came to see the Gandhi again and approached him as he sat below the tree, the great man shouted to him, 'Take care and do not get hurt by the branch!' The missionary felt that such personal concern for others' problems, while busy with national politics at the highest level, was a quality he did not see in any other leader.

Such are the pictures that all his friends and disciples carry in their hearts — the picture of a simple old man bearing superhuman burdens and responsibilities and of grief and pain, but to his friends and colleagues always courteous and tolerant, always understanding, always with a joyful laugh bubbling up from under the surface. 'Come and show me where I am wrong', he would say to his friends and critics. For he was always eager for new truth and always open to conviction. But how hard he was to convince.

Another fascinating aspect of the Mahatma was the manner in which he utilized his followers. He never asked them to do anything which they could not do, if they lacked inspiration. And he inspired them. He did not force them beyond their power to perform, but he led them. His own integrity aroused the response of those whom he led. No wonder John Gunther, the eminent journalist, referred to the Mahatma as a mixture of 'Political Boss, Jesus Christ and Your Father'.

The Title Maharajas Could Not Buy

Among the 565 Indian princes of the British era, the prefix, 'His Highness', to the ruler's other long titles was considered the most desirable and important. The stratagems, devices and efforts the rajas (who did not have the right to be called His Highness) employed to gain this title, provide an interesting insight into human nature.

Contrary to popular belief, Indian rulers were not automatically entitled to the prefix, 'His Highness'. Till 1870, there was no hard and fast rule regarding this and all over India, potentates were addressed by various titles such as His Excellency and so on. But after 1870, the Government of India decided that the title of His Highness would be restricted to important rulers and informed all the British Residents at the princely courts that no Indian ruler who was not entitled to a gun salute of 11 or more, should be allowed the privilege of being called His Highness.

Just after the first World War, the Government of India decided to go into the question of 'His Highness' once again, mainly because they saw in it a means to reward the various Indian rulers who had helped in the war effort. Secondly, the

Indian Government decided that other than certain Indian rulers, the title of His Highness should not be given officially to any other British-Indian subject.

The suggestions made by various officials of the Indian political Department (which dealt with the maharajas), makes interesting reading. The Resident from Mysore drew the attention of the Government of India to the fact that the Maharaja of Mysore (a 21 gun salute State) was allowing his younger brother, the Yuvaraja, to be called His Highness, despite frequent remonstrations from the Resident. He also pointed out that in 1915, when invitation cards for the Yuvaraja's wedding were printed, describing him as His Highness the Yuvaraja of Mysore, the Resident had 'directed' the State to 'withdraw' the cards. Nevertheless, the administration report of Mysore State continued to describe the Yuvaraja as His Highness.

The Residents at the Courts of the Nizam of Hyderabad and the Gaekwar of Baroda, reported that both these potentates wanted their sons to be described as Princes and His Highnesses. An examination of this practice revealed that they were hoping thereby to acquire for themselves an even higher title, that of His Princely Highness or His Illustrious Highness or His Imperial Highness. Further, the Nizam of Hyderabad was very unhappy with his title, as it merely designated him as His Highness. He had pointed out that the hereditary ruler of his Arab soldiers, the Sultan of Shehr and Makalla, in Arabia, was also referred to as His Highness. Hence, he wanted some additional title that would indicate he was above the normal run of Indian rulers.

Together with this title arose the question of whom among the wives of the ruling princes (entitled to the suffix His Highness) were to be termed Her Highness. For example, it was found that the family of the Raja of Tanjore consisted of 11 wives and all of them wanted the title of Her Highness.

Finally, it was decided that the suffix would be applicable only to 'those of the ladies, who had undergone the most regular and orthodox form of marriage and not any inferior or less recognised ceremony'. Then again, in the cases of States like Travancore and Cochin, where the matriarchal system was followed, it was found improper to give the title of Her Highness to the wife of the ruler. In these cases, it was decided that the senior most female member of the family should be called Her Highness.

It was often found that the usual criterion of jurisdictional status, family, number of salutes, income and population were not uniformly applicable to all cases. For example, the Maharana of Udaipur was comparatively less affluent and his State much smaller than that of his neighbours. Yet, as the 'Sun of the Maharajas of Rajasthan', he had to be placed on a high pedestal. Similarly, it was found that the ruler of the State of Manipur had been omitted from the list of maharajas entitled to be called His Highness, just because he seldom

Her Highness the Begum of Bhopal

came out of his State and there was no occasion for him to use his gun salute, which was less than eleven.

The Begum of Bhopal, a premier Indian ruler, focussed another problem as it was not possible to grant her husband the title of His Highness. In Bombay, the title of His Highness the Aga Khan (the religious head of the Ismaili Muslims), was another problem, for he was a dignitary without any ruling powers or territory. Later, the Aga Khan tried to rectify this lacuna by buying the port of Gwadar and its adjacent areas from the Nawab of Baluchistan, but his efforts did not succeed. Further, only those rulers who had the title of His Highness, were entitled to return visits from the Viceroy.

Even when it came to the question of rewarding the princes for their war efforts, it was found that the addition of any honour to the seniormost amongst them, the Nizam, would cause problems, as all the Indian rulers with the same number of gun salutes (21), would ask for the same title.

Finally, it was decided that the Nizam would be called His Exalted Highness and the title of 'Faithful Ally of the British', was added to his list of honours in an autographed letter from His Majesty the King-Emperor. In the case of the Yuvaraja of Mysore, it was decided that, as a special concession, the then Yuvaraja would be allowed the title of His Highness but future Yuvaraja were forbidden to use this title.

Still dissatisfied, the Nizam even wanted for himself the title of His Majesty, but the British Government firmly vetoed the idea. In fact, the British never allowed the maharajas to describe themselves as the Royal Family or as Royal Highnesses. This title was only meant for members of the British Royal Family. The Indian rulers had to be satisfied with calling themselves Durbar or Samasthans and their thrones were referred to as 'Gaddis' or 'Musnuds', depending on the ruler's Hindu or Muslim background. They were not allowed to have coronets with closed points similar to the European crowns and in many cases, when during official functions, the ceremonial tent of the Indian princes was marked as the Royal Pavilion, the British Residents insisted on the word Royal being removed.

This craze to acquire the title of His Highness and more bitterly, the fact that only the first wife of the Indian rulers were usually called Her Highness, led to comical situations. When the Maharaja of Baroda married a second wife, a divorcee, the Viceroy refused point blank to give her the title of Her Highness and instructed the British Resident at Baroda to keep away from the functions where the 'new' rani was present. Similar was the case of the Spanish Maharani of Patiala, who was not to be greeted as Her Highness in any official function.

This general desire for the title of Her Highness, led to a very curious and humorous situation in 1947, as Lord Mountbatten, the last Viceroy of India, sat in his chambers during the night of August 14, when India was to be declared an independent sovereign State, free of the British Empire. All confidential files had been despatched to London and there was nothing more for the Viceroy to do as he sat awaiting the stroke of the clock at midnight with his A.D.Cs nearby. As he fidgetted in his seat, Lord Mountbatten suddenly began to smile. What was to be the final act of the last Viceroy of India? He remembered that his friend, the Nawab of Palanpur, had long requested him to give his Begum (wife) the title of Her Highness. Palanapur was not a 11 gun salute State and therefore, the Viceroy could not agree to the request, lest it upset the protocol among the Indian rulers. But once the Empire has passed into history, nobody could change the given titles, nor could anyone be given any new titles to correct the 'errors'. Laughingly, Lord Mountbatten asked for his official seal and letterhead as the Viceroy of India and had the Begum of Palanpur invested with the title of Her Highness and affixed the Viceroy's signature and official seal on the document. This was therefore the last act of the Viceroy of India as he passed into history.

The Greatest Plunder in History

In centuries gone by, the Mongols had laid waste the Chinese Empire, the Huns had despoiled the Roman nation and the Spaniards had plundered the Aztecs of America. But materially, all these acts of vandalism combined, did not equal Nadir Shah's sack of the Mughal capital of Delhi in 1739, when in the words of a contemporary chronicler, 'The accumulated wealth of 348 years changed hands in three days'.

Nadir Kuli (meaning Slave of the Wonderful [God]), was born the son of Imam Kuli, a humble member of the sheep rearing Khirklu tribe in the Khorasan area of Persia. In 1688 AD Nadir Kuli entered the service of the local Governor and won his master's favour by rescuing his family from marauders. The Governor, to permanently secure the allegiance of this intrepid young man, made him his son-in-law and eventually, Nadir Kuli succeeded the Governor in that august post. A series of effective military campaigns elevated him to the rank of Commander-in-Chief of the Persian Army and when 1732 AD, the Persian Emperor lost vast portions of the Empire to the Turks, Nadir Kuli deposed him and ascended the throne as Nadir Shah, in 1736.

Nadir Shah's ambition was to emulate Alexander the Great and Timur the Terrible as world conquerors but he knew that the Persian treasury would not be able to support these grandiose plans. The only alternative was to acquire the wealth of his neighbour, the Mughal Emperor Muhammad Shah and as a prelude to the invasion, Nadir Shah sent frequent complaints to the Mughal Court, that they were granting asylum to Persian rebels. Muhammad Shah knew that the border with the Persian Empire was sparsely guarded. But, in the weakened state of his empire, there was nothing he could do except bargain for time. Nadir Shah meanwhile collected 40,000 soldiers and crossed the Punjab with swift marches. The Mughal marshalled his cumbersome army numbering 75,000, to meet the invader. The battle at Karnal, 60 miles from Delhi, lasted two and half hours and the Persians emerged victorious while the Mughal forces left behind 12,000 dead in the field.

Nizam-ul-Mulk, the Viceroy of the Deccan and the doyen amongst Mughal nobles, asked his suzerain to sue for peace and offered to serve as messenger to the Persian conqueror. Nadir Shah, whose hero worship of Timur the Terrible, was remarkable, did not want to humiliate or murder the Mughal Emperor, the lineal descendant of Timur and agreed to Nizam-ul-Mulk's entreaties that he should return to Persia, if an indemnity of five million silver rupees was paid to him. Glad to escape at such a cheap price, Muhammad Shah agreed and on the second day after his defeat, went to the Persian camp to pay his respects to the conqueror.

Normally, the Persian would have returned to his capital without further plundering the Mughal Empire. But traitorous rivalry, the bane of the Mughal Empire, entered the scene in the person of Saadat Khan, the Viceroy of Oudh. This powerful noble felt that the success of Nizam-ul-Mulk in turning away the invader from Delhi, would make him the Emperor's favourite adviser and this he wished to prevent.

Therefore, Saadat Khan approached Nadir Shah and told him that the Persians had been outwitted by the Mughal noble and that if Nadir Shah captured Delhi, he could carry away as booty 500 million rupees, a hundred times the amount offered by the Mughal Emperor.

Nadir Shah required no further goading and proceeded to imprison the Mughal Emperor and Nizam-ul-Mulk in his camp before demanding a ransom of 200 million rupees. The aged Mughal noble pleaded in vain that there never was 200 million rupees in the Mughal treasury in a single day. In the previous century Emperor Shah Jahan had collected 160 million rupees as treasure in his coffers and the whole amount had been spent by his son Emperor Aurangazeb for his wars and that it was going to be difficult to raise even the five million rupees he had offered to the Persians.

But it was too late to quench the Persian's avarice and he marched onto Delhi with the royal prisoner. It is only fair to add that, soon after, Nizam-ul-Mulk had the traitor Saadat Khan murdered through a stratagem. Entering Delhi, Nadir Shah took over the Empire, minted coins in his name and had the *khutba* (prayers) recited in his own name as the Emperor of India. As the Mughal Emperor's ransom, he claimed the whole of the Mughal Treasury and further, the capital of Delhi was assessed at 20 million rupees, if it was to escape looting by Nadir Shah's troops.

The Peacock Throne of the Mughals, the most fabulous treasure in history, was of course the first in the list of pillaged items. Legends allude that the Mughal was unwilling to hand over the famous Kohinoor diamond, as myths had averred that as long as he kept the famous diamond with him, he would regain the throne as the Emperor of India. In order to prevent the Persian from snatching it, the Mughal hid it in his turban. But Nadir Shah had his own information regarding the Mughal jewels and when, during the course of parleys, he offered to exchange his turban with that of the Mughal Emperor, as a mark of friendship, the hapless Muhammad Shah had no choice but to do so and the Kohinoor diamond changed hands.

According to Sir Jadunath Sarkar, the eminent historian, the value of the gold, silver and cash taken away by the invader, was estimated at 300 million rupees; the jewels at 250 million; the Peacock Throne and nine other thrones and several weapons, all worked with precious stones, were estimated at 90 million rupees, rich manufactures in the shape of art objects and famous silks, at 20 million rupees and cannon, stores and furniture, at 40 million rupees. In all, a total of 700 million rupees. As the British pound in those days was worth 8.8 Indian rupees, this loot can be assessed at 80 million lb sterling. According to Bank of England, the British pound then was worth 66 times the 1995 pound in terms of purchasing power. In today's monetary value, Nadir Shah took away 5,280 million lb sterling worth of booty from Delhi.

Besides this, the Persian claimed as war booty, 300 elephants, 10,000 horses and 10,000 camels, in addition to innumerable other baggage animals.

Further, to ensure everlasting alliance between the two monarchs, Nadir Shah's son and the Mughal's daughter were married in a grand ceremony. The Mughal resented this unwanted alliance with a shepherd more than the loss of his wealth. When Nadir Shah was informed that the bridegroom's geneaology over seven generations must be known to finalize the marriage, he brusquely replied, 'He is the son of Nadir Shah, the son of the Sword, the grandson of the Sword and so on to seventy instead of seven generations.'

During the initial weeks, Nadir Shah's well disciplined army seems to have conducted itself with restraint. But as the grain stocks in Delhi became low, Nadir Shah seized the granaries and fixed a fair price system to prevent profiteering. The grain merchants, then as now, protested against this fixed price and the resulting tension ended in a burst of rioting. Meanwhile, rumours went round the city that the Mughal Emperor's harem guards had assassinated Nadir Shah and thus emboldened, the citizens of Delhi began killing the Persian soldiers.

These killings, together with the grain rioting, angered Nadir Shah and when he found that nearly 3,000 of his troops had been killed, he ordered a general massacre. He took his seat in the courtyard of the Roshan-ud-Dowlah Mosque at Chandni Chowk (the jeweller's street of Delhi), to supervise the reprisals. Between sunrise and the afternoon of March 22, 1739, more than 20,000 citizens were massacred by the Persian soldiers and finally, the aged noble Nizam-ul-Mulk, pleaded with the Persian to desist. Nadir Shah sheathed his sword exclaiming, 'For the sake of thy grey beard I forgive'. Ever since that day, the main city gate near Chandni Chowk has been known as Khuni Darwaza (Gate of Blood) and in local parlance, a *nadir shahi* means a massacre.

All the Persian soldiers were rewarded generously by Nadir Shah. They were given 18 months' salary (one third as arrears, one third as advance and one third as bounty) and the Generals of the Persian Army were lavishly rewarded. The rich treasure he carried with him would have sufficed to change the history of Persia if it had been wisely spent. Instead, the very treasure proved to be Nadir Shah's undoing. As a gift to his people after the capture of Delhi, he had excused three years taxes throughout Persia. But soon afterwards, with incredible folly, he cancelled the orders and asked his tax collectors to realise the dues fully. The Persian populace, unable to understand the sudden change in the concession, fought the tax collectors and by the time the

Persian Treasury collected the amount, Nadir Shah's name became a curse to his own subjects. Finally, unable to bear his cruelties, Nadir Shah's own commanders rose against him and murdered him during one of his campaigns, in 1747.

In far-off Delhi, the treasury was literally empty, the populace had lost faith in Mughal arms and the whole empire broke up into independent kingdoms. In fact, historians trace the fall of the Mughal Empire from the date of Nadir Shah's departure.

When Indian Patriots Wanted an Indian Officer Corps for the Indian Army

The Sepoy Mutiny convinced the British of two facts — that they could not hold India without Indian soldiers and that it would be foolhardy to develop an Indian officer Corps to command the Indian Army. For, the Mutiny was quelled by the British not because of the superiority of the British Tommy over the Indian sepoy, but due to the fact that the rebel sepoys did not have trained military officers to lead them. It is certainly true that in the High Command of the Sepoy Army, there were many powerful personalities like the Rani of Jhansi who possessed great military flair, the shrewd Tantia Topi, who excelled mostly in guerrilla warfare and General Bhakt Khan (who restored the sepoy garrison in Delhi to a semblance of discipline) and whom the British called the most capable commander the Mughal Emperor had. But these gifted but pathetically few leaders at the top, were no substitute for the lack of trained and military-oriented officers at the lower level, to lead the ranks of rebel Sepoy Army, which numbered 45 regiments at its peak.

In the words of Sir John Lawrence, a famous British administrator, 'In many instances the mutineers seemed to act as if a curse rested on their cause. Nay. Had they followed any other course than that they did pursue in many instances, we the British must have been lost beyond redemption. The Sepoys fought valiantly and often courageously, but without leadership and without the self-confidence and determination, which sustained the British, the mutineer's cause became hopeless. Weak British garrisons were left unmolested, elementary precautions like demolition of bridges overlooked, large bodies like the Gwalior contingent of rebel sepoys left idle and the sepoys were left to worry about individual grievances'. Thus the Indian sepoys, bereft of an Officers Corps, never made effective use of those advantages which they did possess, especially in early stages of the revolt.

If they had marched to Calcutta instead of Delhi, the course of the Mutiny would have been different. Indeed, once free of British authority, the sepoy rarely knew what to do. The British officers leading their army into Delhi on September 11, 1857, were moved by the courageous fight the rebel sepoy put up, but sickened by the untrained manner he let go of his advantages since he had no officers to lead him.

Thus, aware that creating a class of Indian officers would spell ruin for them, the British steadfastly refused to have an Indian Officers Corps. They realized that there was excellent officer material available in the Indian ranks. In fact, in Clive's army of the previous century, there had been many Indian and Eurasian commanders. Sir Munro, in 1817, had deplored the policy of having no Indian officers when they were available. In 1847, Sir Henry Lawrence, had written in one of his reports: 'While for the lower ranks, service in the Company's

Army is a splendid one, it offers no inducement to superior intellects or more shining spirits. Men so endowed leave us in disgust and rise to rank in foreign services. There are many commandants in the Maratha and Sikh Services, who were just privates in the Company's Army.' The historian, Kaye, mentions that the East India Company at one stage wanted to employ Indian officers from the top echelons of Indian society. But they were not able to take early action and the Mutiny changed the course of their thinking and under the British Government, the Queen's Commission was to be given to European/British subjects only and Indian applicants had to be content with the Viceroy's Commission.

But the British were also aware that, as political fervour began to seethe in India, they would be unable to retain posts in the Indian Army Officer Corps as the preserve of the British and at one stage, the British thought to use the lure of these military posts to counterpoise the political desires of the intelligentsia. Lord George Hamilton, the Secretary of State for India, wrote in 1897, 'If we can keep the affection of the fighting races and higher orders of society in India, we can ignore the dislike and disaffection of intellectual non-fighting races, the *baboos*, the students and the pleaders.'

Opposed to such liberal thinking were the many diehards in British officialdom, who felt that as far as the Indian Army was concerned, Queen Victoria's Proclamation of 1858, assuring equality of opportunity, should be considered a dead letter. This view was reinforced by the opinion of one of the top British commanders, Lord Roberts, who opined that the consciousness of the inherent superiority of Europeans had won for the British the Indian Empire and that it was dangerous to have a nucleus of highly trained Indian officers in the Army, who might lead the sepoys against the British.

Despite the odds, in 1885, twenty-eight years after the Mutiny, General Chesney requested the Viceroy to suggest to the British Government that it would be advisable to encourage talent amongst Indians by initially having only two regiments led by Indian officers. But the coterie of Colonel Blimps surrounding the Secretary of State vetoed the idea and the same fate befell Lord Kitchener's (the then C-in-C of the Indian Army) proposals twenty years later. This time, the scheme was killed by the Viceroy, Lord Curzon, who felt that military education should be confined to the small class of nobility or gentry. But World War I (1914-18) enforced the necessity of using the best talent available and many Indians were commissioned in the British Army and the Royal Flying Corps College, at Cranwell.

But once the war was over, the same imperialist spirit returned and Indianisation was throttled back because it would diminish the opportunities available to demobilised officers of the British Army, who would like to join the Indian Army. Illustrative of the lame excuses offered was that given by Sir O'Moore Creagh, who stated that if Indian officers were recruited, 'Social integration would be prevented by the fact that English ladies would not like to associate with the wives of Indian officers, whose social position was not clear'. Another favourite argument was that the British officer should not be asked to serve under Indian officers and that the fighting races like the Sikhs and Mahsuds would never agree to be led in battle by the bookish Bengali and Madrasi officers. The British generals also had noticed earlier that the British officers who had fraternized with their Indian colleagues at Sandhurst and Cranwell, were not willing to mix with them in India. Another fear expressed by the British top brass was that British officers would oppose their sons taking up careers in the Indian Army, were they asked to serve under Indians.

But by this time, the cause for Indian young men to lead their own army, had powerful votaries like Pandit Motilal

Nehru, who felt that the problems were not that of Indianizing but that of getting rid of Europeanisation. He strongly advocated the King's Commission for Indian officers. He succintly told the British that the aura of martial races was a myth created by them and it was silly to talk of an Army leadership that would be bereft of the intelligentsia provided by the so-called non-martial races. He further pointed out, that according to even British historians, it was the so-called non-martial races of Bengali, Madrasi and United Provinces soldiery, who helped the British conquer India and not the Sikhs and Mahsuds. As for the Mahsuds not accepting Indian leadership, Motilal Nehru sarcastically commented that the Mahsud had not accepted the British either and that in any case, British leadership in the North Western Frontier Provinces, the homeland of the Mahsuds, was not worth emulating. General Thimmayya, later to be the Commander-in-Chief of the Indian Army after Indian independence feelingly mentions in his memoirs the grand part played by Motilal Nehru in the Indianisation of the Officer Corps.

By 1918, the Commander-in-Chief of the Indian Army, Lord Rawlinson, felt that the Officer Corps of the Indian Army should be rapidly Indianised and his efforts failed as the British Government did not take kindly to his suggestions. By 1922, the same Commander-in-Chief felt that it would take 30 years to complete the process of Indianisation.

On March 2, 1921, Indian nationalists in the Central Legislature tabled the following resolutions for immediate action:
1) Indians be admitted in commissioned ranks of the Royal Artillery, Royal Engineers and the Royal Air Force.
2) The number of commissions granted to Indians be immediately raised to twenty five per cent of the annual commissions given to the Indian Army.
3) Immediate steps to be taken to establish an Indian Military Academy.

The Government of India, thus shocked into action by the fervour of the Indian leaders, placed the proposals before the British Government which summarily rejected the schemes.

But the ferment that had set in was too intense to be thus bypassed and a committee headed by Lt. General Sir Andrew Skeen, Chief of General Staff in India and having amongst its members, Motilal Nehru and M.A. Jinnah (founder of Pakistan), was formed to investigate the question of:
1) Steps to be taken for the establishment of a Military College in India for Indian Commissioned Officers for the Indian Army.
2) Where a Military college should be established in India? When established, should it supercede or supplement the Military Colleges at Woolwich and Sandhurst?
3) At what rate should Indianisation be accelerated in order to attract Indians to a military career.

The Skeen Committee recommended that the number of vacancies for Indian cadets at Sandhurst be increased from 10 to 12 and that a further number of 10 Viceroy's Commissioned Officers of Indian origin, be sent to Sandhurst for training every year. It also stated that while the percentage of Indian officers should be increased, it would not be at the cost of Army efficiency and (what is more important), not by diminishing the supply of British recruits to commissioned ranks in the Indian Army. As a result of the Skeen Committee recommendations, an Indian Sandhurst Committee was set up and this Committee (with Messrs Motilal Nehru and Jinnah among its members), toured France, UK and Canada to finalise the decision on an Indian Sandhurst. Thus prodded by Indian nationalists, the Indian Military Academy was established at Dehradun in 1932 and by 1939, ten per cent of the Officer Corps of the Indian Army were Indians. Further, by 1938, the Government of India had made it its stable policy to have as peace time recruitment, one third of the

Officer Corps constituted by Indian young men.

When the World War II broke out, the Government of India found that to man the two million strong Indian Army (the World's largest voluntary army), they did not have sufficient officers and recruited four hundred young Indians in a hurry, giving them King's Commissions. The war gave a great impetus to the Indianization of the Officer Corps and when it ended, there were nearly 8,000 Indian officers in the Indian Army, comprising 20 per cent of the Officer Corps and there were another 1,000 Indian officers in the Navy and the Air Force. The World War II ended once and for all the myth of martial races and proved that the Indian Army did not have to depend only on the 'nobility and gentry' to supply its officers. The Indian middle class, with its intelligentsia, was well able to take care of the wonderful *Jawan*, the sophisticated machinery and scientific equipment of modern warfare.

Indian Independence, Nehru and Hitler

By a strange quirk of fate, 1989 marked the birth centenary year for two titans of the 20th century — Adolf Hitler being born on April 20, 1889 and Jawaharlal Nehru on November 14, 1889. But their impact on world history differed as much as the proverbial chalk and cheese. Now, more than five decades after Hitler's suicide and three decades after Nehru's demise, many hitherto 'top secret' documents in the national archives of Germany, Britain and India have been thrown open to scholars and through the researches of historians like Milan Hauner, Heiber, S. Gopal and Dorothy Norman, we can evaluate the interaction between these two leaders and their opinions regarding each other.

Strangely enough, the cause of Indian independence, in Nehru's case, his life's crusade and on Hitler's part (a strange manifestation of his love-hate relationship with the British) a desire to perpetuate the British hegemony forever over the subcontinent, proved to be the 'boxing ring' where these two famous figures of history collided. This antagonism was made more complicated and for Nehru more 'painful', due to the pro-German tilt of Subhas Chandra Bose, eight years junior to him but almost his equal where the adulation of the Indian masses was concerned.

Indian nationalists in the first four decades of the present century, did harbour a secret admiration for the disciplined German nation (a natural counterpoise to the British imperial power) and German scholars showed great interest in ancient Indian philosophy and science. It was hoped that the might of Germany would prove to be the key that would unlock India's British shackles.

But scholars like H. Trevor-Roper (in his book *Hitler's Table Talks*), reveals that, despite his antipathy towards the British nation, Hitler had no intention of aiding India's liberation. In fact, he was solely obsessed with the idea that the British, whom he admired fanatically for the their conquest of India, should never leave India. In 1942, after the Japanese conquered South East Asia, occupying Singapore, Hitler pensively discussed with his Generals, what he would have done(if he had been in the place of the British) and decided that he would have concluded a separate Peace Treaty with Japan to preserve India as *the* British colony. As far as the Indian freedom movement was concerned, he criticized the British for their parleys with Congress leaders.

Nehru had visited Germany before the rise of Hitler to power. In those days, bereft of its colonies after World War I, Germany was inclined to be friendly towards anti-colonialists. In fact, the famous convention, the Congress of Oppressed Nationalities, held in Brussels in 1927, took shape from discussions between groups of anti-imperialist sympathisers in Berlin. While he was in Berlin in 1927, Nehru learned of the forthcoming Congress and attended as the delegate from the Indian National Congress. Under his guidance, the propaganda wing of the Indian organisation, known as the Indian Information Bureau, was established in Berlin, in 1929. But as soon as the Nazi tide overwhelmed Germany, the new German Government's sympathy for 'oppressed nationalities' vanished. In 1933, the Nazi party under Hitler, had the Indian Information Bureau closed down, as Hitler commanded the closure of all such 'anti-colonial' organisations. Nehru's aide in Germany, A.C. Nambiar, who headed the Bureau, had his house raided by the Gestapo and he himself was ordered to leave Germany.

Nine years later, in 1942, Subhas Chandra Bose asked Hitler's permission for Nambiar to return to Germany, to enable him to assist the Indian leader's efforts to free India. When Nambiar professed reluctance to becoming an aide to Bose after being Nehru's disciple, Bose had one simple answer, 'What you want to do is to serve the cause of Indian freedom. If the Allies win the war, then there would be your leader Nehru to take India to freedom and if the Axis win, then I would be the Supremo. As such you will always be able to serve India.' It is poignant to note that A.C. Nambiar lived to serve independent India as the country's Ambassador to Germany.

When they found that by the 1930s, Nehru had become the most popular nationalist leader in India after the Mahatma, the Nazi Government made informal approaches to him, hoping to induce him to visit Germany as their 'guest'. Nehru refused and when staying in Munich, Germany, as a private tourist in 1938, declined to meet any Nazi official. Further, after his visit to Czechoslovakia, his statement that, 'Czechoslovakia was being raped by Germany, while Britain and France were holding the Czech nation on the ground to facilitate the rape', did not endear him to the Nazis.

Documents from the Nazi Germany archives show that Hitler's 'India Cell' was closely monitoring the attitude of the Indian National Congress towards world events and according to them, Nehru was pro-Soviet, while Bose was the 'friend' of Germany. In fact, as World War II progressed, the pro-Axis tilt of Bose and the pro-Allies (rather pro-Democracy) sympathy shown by Nehru, was to cause worry to their common mentor, Mahatma Gandhi, that the Indian freedom movement might get 'split' between these two eminent nationalists.

Nehru himself was keenly observing the German political situation and strangely enough, was in Europe during the crucial stages of the Nazi terror sweeping Europe. He was present in the British Parliament when Chamberlain addressed the House prior to leaving for Munich and was depressed to find that Chamberlain was not the 'Man' for the occasion. Commenting on the clash between Chamberlain and Hitler, Nehru wrote in his newspaper, *National Herald*, 'My thoughts flew to his (Chamberlain's) meeting with Hitler and I thought how overwhelmed he must have been by Hitler, overwhelmed not only by the frequent ultimatums of the latter, but by the dynamic and passionate and somewhat neurotic personality. For Hitler, for all his evil bent and distorted intent, has something elemental about him and Mr. Chamberlain is of the earth — earthy. But even Mr. Chamberlain could have met that elemental force, with another force, also elemental, but far more powerful, the force of organised Democracy, the Will of the millions of people. He did not possess that power, nor did he seek to possess it'.

Despite his abhorence of Hitler's fascist methods, Nehru genuinely tried to 'understand him'. An entry in his *Prison Diary* dated July 24, 1941, reads thus, 'Yesterday I finished reading Hitler's *Mein Kampf*, a full and unexpurgated edition. Previously, when Hitler seized power in 1933, I had read long extracts from the book and had formed a very unfavourable opinion of it and its author. What struck me particularly was an element of vulgarity about him. I must say that I have been impressed by the book now'.

Hitler had his own estimate of Nehru and he always liked to compare Nehru with Subhash Chandra Bose. In his recorded table talks (researched by Milan Hauner), after hearing about the escape of Bose from India to the Axis Camp, Hitler welcomed the news and stated, 'Now, that man of compromise, Nehru, has been eclipsed by Bose'.

The famous and only meeting of Bose with Hitler took place in the German dictator's mountain retreat, The Wolf's Lair, on May 27, 1942. He told Bose that he did not believe that the anti-fascist bent of Nehru and Gandhi's theory of passive resistance, would be of any consequence in the long run. Ironically, Hitler was not even willing to issue a 'Declaration of Independence to Indian People' freeing India if the Axis won the war. An old revolutionary himself, he advised Bose that he should go to seek the help of Japan. Japanese forces had reached the borders of India and Hitler felt that British rule in India could only be broken by a simultaneous internal revolution in India alongwith the military thrust of the Axis. In fact, the only help Hitler offered was a submarine to take Bose to a Japanese controlled area in South East Asia.

In India, Bose's escape to Germany had made the ideological lines clearer and Nehru too did not mince words. Earlier, on January 3, 1942, he had stated in Bombay, during a press conference, 'We have no sympathy with Hitler. We are under no illusion that he will give us our freedom'.

What followed after the end of World War II is now history now. But one can be sure that the world could not have realised in 1889, that of these two infants born in the same year, one would become the chief disciple of the Mahatma, the world's greatest apostle of non-violence and the other would terrorise humanity as history's most ruthless exponent of violence.

British Ghosts Continue to Haunt India

Though the British left India in 1947, their ghosts continued to haunt India as late as 1988. In the hill station of Ooty, in south India, Mrs Carter (1902-90) lived adjacent to the 160-year-old St. Stephen's Church. Mrs. Carter must have been one of the oldest British citizens alive in India and had first come to India as the young bride of a tea planter, in 1919 when she was seventeen. In her cottage, Mrs. Carter led a quiet life and when we met in early 1988, confided that her house must be more than one hundred-years old — one of the earliest buildings in Ooty. Mrs. Carter further disclosed that, in her well-maintained gardens, she had often seen the apparition of a well-dressed British lady, most probably the earlier occupant of the house, who apparently still loved the garden well enough to pay occasional visits. 'The apparition is very quiet and harmless, except for scaring away dogs in the vicinity'. When I was checking through records in UK, a retired Army officer, Major General Moberly, remarked that he had read somewhere that a distant relation, a Mrs. Moberly, was reputed to haunt her house in Ooty. As local historians in Ooty were unable to tell me of any other house in Ooty haunted by a lady, perhaps Mrs. Carter's 'occasional ghost visitor' could be Mrs. Moberly.

The British are known to have a great fascination for ghosts, which is probably one reason why some of them who died in India between 1600 and 1947, are said to haunt their former residences. According to one British historian's estimate, no less than two million citizens of Great Britain — soldiers, administrators, doctors, planters, missionaries and so on, had died in India during 347 years. It is therefore expected as in 'Olde England', where a castle is not considered respectable unless it has a ghost to haunt it, that there are British who haunt their old dwellings, be it in the salubrious cantonment of Poona or the once malaria-ridden plantations of southern and north eastern India. Even the city of Calcutta, the capital of British India for more than 150 years, is not free.

Lady Reading, the Vicereine of India in 1920s, refers to the famous Ridge at Delhi, as the 'place, where there were English ghosts among all the Hindu, Central Asian, Mahratha and Afghan spectres'. As a battlefield between India sepoys and British soldiers in 1857, the Ridge had a particularly eerie reputation in the evenings, at the turn of the century and in the officer's quarter over the main gate of the Red Fort, where British forces had been massacred in 1857, even the stolid garrison gunners in the 20th century felt uneasy.

Inside the Red Fort, where, in the initial days of the 1857 uprising, a number of British ladies and children had been brutally killed under a tree in the courtyard of the Diwan-i-Am it is said that horses would shy away from the spot under the tree for decades after the massacre.

Meerut, as the British cantonment where the Sepoy

Mutiny started, had a number of houses with plaques affixed to their facades, telling of British officers and their families who had been killed during the struggle. In the course of the oral history sessions conducted by the BBC for its *Recollections of the Raj*, one British Army officer's wife told the interviewer that, during the early decades of the present century, there were a number of old regimental houses in Meerut, in which no dog would enter — a sure sign of ghost haunting. Nobody could sleep at night inside these houses due to banging doors, blasts of chilly wind and similar manifestations. Often, the officers and their families had to spread their bedding on cots in the compound to get some undisturbed rest.

Hill stations had their own sad saga of ghosts. Arriving at one of the official houses allotted to their family in Simla, one British memsahib found the bedroom haunted by a wraith-like apparition. Recounting the tale to the BBC oral history team in the 1970s, the old lady (then in her seventies) said that on enquiring with the old gardener, she was told that a young army wife had committed suicide in one of the rooms. The lady decided to confront the ghost and went to the churchyard, where the unfortunate woman had been buried. Standing before the grave, she addressed the ghost sternly, 'You have given me very unpleasant moments'.

As mentioned earlier, Ooty, then considered the 'Queen of Hill Stations' in southern India, had its quota of ghosts and one such spectre was well known in the 170-year-old *Glenview* bungalow, the present headquarters of the Untied Planters' Association of South India (known as the UPASI) in Coonoor, a hill station close to Ooty.

I met one of the former Secretaries to the UPASI some time ago and the gentleman (then nearing 80) mentioned that the ghost was said to be that of the owner of a series of buildings, of which *Glenview* (then a hotel) was a part. In the early

1930s, unable to meet his liabilities, the hotel owner, a British citizen committed suicide. Later, haunting his former hotel as a ghost, he engaged in nothing more annoying than physically 'transferring' guests from one room to another during the night, without their being aware of the movement. You might have gone to sleep in the western bedroom only to wake up in the northern hall. The gentleman's wife confided that, on occasion, when she had been seriously ill, she had seen the ghost looking 'like an old durzi (tailor) with a night cap on his head', standing by her bedside. What made her expect the ghost on such occasion was the phenomenon of the room getting extraordinarily 'chilly', even for the cool hill station. A few years ago, the portion of *Glenview* which housed the ghost, was burnt down, thus writing *finis* to the ghost's career. The newly constructed annexe seems to be free of this nocturnal visitor.

As quoted in one of the articles in the *Planter's Chronicle*, a journal published by the UPASI, 'There is a white house covered with honeysuckle in the Nilgiris in south India, which was once the home of a British tea planter called Colonel Pascoe, a bachelor, who was 80 when he died. He left behind a beautifully kept tea estate and a house called *Woodland*, which his ghost is said to haunt. This habit is highly disconcerting for his Indian successors as on the first night a guest moves in, the ghost can be heard noisily counting gold sovereigns in a huge safe, which is kept locked. He then glides across the highly polished wooden floor and nudges the new arrival out of his bed, ruffling the mosquito net.' The Colonel's old servant Joseph, still worked in the house in 1980, shuffling around in wide beige shoes. 'Sometimes when I dust the master's room, he taps me on the arm and tries to push me away', Joseph said, 'But it is not frightening and he always leaves people alone after the first night.'

The hill stations with tea or coffee plantations, housed

hordes of *chota* sahibs (junior managers) and *burra* sahibs (senior managers), who were very often lonely bachelors. Bored with their lonely existence they often led 'drink-sodden' lives. W.Y. Evans-West, in a footnote to the *Tibetan Book of the Dead* says that he heard of a European planter, who having died in the jungles of the Malabar country of southern India, was buried there by the native people. Some years later, a friend of the planter found the grave carefully fenced in and bordered with empty whisky and beer bottles. At a loss to understand such an unusual sight, he asked for an explanation and was told that the dead sahib's ghost had caused much trouble and that an old local witch doctor had found a way out by prescribing whisky and beer for the ghost, stuff to which it had long been habituated when in the flesh. The local people, although religiously opposed to intoxicants, began purchasing bottled whisky and beer of the same brands which the dead sahib had been known to prefer and with a regular ritual for the dead, began sacrificing them to the ghost by pouring the liquor upon the grave. Discovering that this kept the ghost quiet, they kept up the practise. It is said that the bottles continue to accumulate.

According to the writer Heather Lovatt, the *Pambanar* bungalow (in the central hill district of Kerala state), a planter's bungalow which was built in 1912 on the site of an older bungalow, has the distinction of being haunted by two ghosts, one of whom is a horseman who rides up the steps from the garden side of the house. The strange tale runs like this. Robert Imray was the acting manager of the tea estate, the main bungalow of which was known as *Bon Ami*, the hub of the local planter's society.

Frank Crozier, the owner of the estate, died at sea on his way back from leave in England. Frank Crozier's widow married his old friend Robert Imray, who had been the chief witness to the will in which Crozier bequeathed the *Pambanar* estate 'to my beloved wife, Rosa Onslow Leslie Crozier'. On Imray's advice, she sold the estate six years later. It is said that during Crozier's absence from the estate, Imray and Rosa used to rendezvous frequently. According to the old Indian servant Lakshmanan, Imray on his horse and the widowed Roza Crozier, still haunt the estate bungalow in 'nocturnal trysts'.

In Calcutta, the house in which Warren Hastings, the first Governor General of India lived in the 1770s, is still extant, although it now houses a Women Teachers' Training College. For decades, local gardeners used to aver that on New Year's Eve every year, a phantom coach drawn by four horses would emerge from the dark and dashing out of the coach at the portico, the wraithlike figure of Warren Hastings would be seen rushing into the house to search for some items apparently hidden there by him.

It was said that, some of the documents, which would have been of great value in defending himself during his impeachment by the British Parliament in the late 18th century, were kept by him in a secret compartment in one of the writing desks. The desk had been lost and poor Warren Hastings has been in search of the papers ever since. Contemporary 18th century records of the East India Company confirm that Warren Hastings did indeed lose important papers which were kept in a wooden almirah or desk and for the return of which he offered large sums of money. But in vain. As late as the 1930s, Lady Braid-Taylor, wife of the last British Governor of the Reserve Bank of India, Sir Braid-Taylor, residing in the old Hastings house, found it haunted and the ghosts of soldiers wearing the uniform of the 18th century East India Company, scared her child in the master bedroom.

Excerpted from the book "British Ghosts in India" by K.R.N. Swamy and Ms. Meera Ravi. ISBN 81-85796-06-8.